STEELE WASECA
COOPERATIVE ELECTRI

SWCE

Office, Garage and Warehouse Facili

- Architect -
Architectural Design Group
- General Contractor -
Rocon, Incorporated, Owatonna,

Plumbing - McCarthy Plumbing & Heating, Inc., Owatonna, M
Sprinkler - Viking Sprinkler, St. Paul, MN
HVAC - K.S.W. Roofing & Heating, Inc., Owatonna, MN
Electrical - M & M Electrical, Inc., New Richland, MN
Landscaper - Helen's Turf & Tree, Medford, MN

THE POWER OF HUMAN CONNECTIONS
STEELE WASECA CO-OP
ELECTRIC
Office Division

Redeem

MAKING THE
CONNECTION

Steele-Waseca Cooperative Electric, 1936–2011

MAKING THE
CONNECTION

Steele-Waseca Cooperative Electric, 1936–2011

By
Randy Sobrack

Your Touchstone Energy® Partner
The power of human connections

TITLE PAGE IMAGE: Steele-Waseca Cooperative Electric employees pictured in 2010 include (bottom row, left to right): Kim Huxford, Jennifer Wilson, Todd Kubicek, Kathy Friedrichs, Darla DeVries, Laurie Burbank, Cindy Aamot, Kim Wilson, Don Bos, Jon Stelter, Jake Jacobson, Syd Briggs, Paul Hoffman, Debbie Eby, Dave Lundberg, Randy Sobrack, and Doug Hughes. Middle row (L-R): Roger Rehman, Paul Hanson, John Iverson, Mark McDonald, Kristi Robinson, and Jim Wolters. Top row (L-R): Ryan Brockway, Barret McClaskie, Justin Bergeson, Dan Meier, Tom Poole, Troy Pederson, Jack Schwab, and Matt Rohman. Not pictured: Nordean Hartle, Luke Ranvek, and DeAnn Kaplan. (*Photo courtesy of Oldenburg Photography*)

The Donning Company Publishers
184 Business Park Drive, Suite 206
Virginia Beach, VA 23462

Steve Mull, *General Manager*
Barbara Buchanan, *Office Manager*
Anne Burns, *Editor*
Stephanie Danko, *Graphic Designer*
Priscilla Odango, *Imaging Artist*
Tonya Washam, *Marketing Specialist*
Pamela Engelhard, *Marketing Advisor*

John Richardson, *Project Director*

Library of Congress Cataloging-in-Publication Data

Sobrack, Randy, 1963-
	Making the connection : Steele-Waseca Cooperative Electric, 1936/2011 / by Randy Sobrack.
		p. cm.
	Includes bibliographical references and index.
	ISBN 978–1–57864–681–4
1. Steele-Waseca Cooperative Electric—History. 2. Electric cooperatives—Minnesota—History. 3. Electric utilities—Minnesota—History. I. Title.
	HD9685.U7S6988 2011
	334'.681333793209776—dc22

									2011008385

Printed in the United States of America at Walsworth Publishing Company

Contents

Foreword

Steele-Waseca Cooperative Electric is recognizing their first seventy-five years in 2011. From the vision of President Franklin Delano Roosevelt of bringing electricity to rural America, to the grassroots efforts of those who organized and recruited farmers that made this cooperative possible, we recognize their efforts of changing a lifestyle without electricity to the modern conveniences we enjoy today with electric power.

This anniversary book will provide insight as to what life was like without electricity, the building of a cooperative when the country was struggling with the effects of the Great Depression and subsequently World War II, the growth that came from the discovered benefits and affordability of electricity, to the challenges of meeting demands for electricity as our country is changing and keeping the lights on when Mother Nature had different ideas.

Many men and women have contributed to the success of Steele-Waseca in seventy-five years including line workers, groundmen, construction crews, office staff, general managers, and boards of directors. Steele-Waseca has been dedicated to our membership and the principles of being a cooperative. The principles of our predecessors have guided our decisions to the present and will continue to do so in the future. ■

Syd Briggs
General Manager

Donald R. Kolb
Board President

Acknowledgments

The development of this book was made possible by General Manager Syd Briggs, the Steele-Waseca Cooperative Electric Board of Directors, and the anniversary book committee.

Steele-Waseca Cooperative Electric wishes to acknowledge the construction crews, contractors, tree services, law enforcement, fire departments, and fellow cooperatives and utilities, along with the farmers who assisted our co op during its first seventy-five years (to attempt to list everyone would risk omitting someone). Your efforts allowed Steele-Waseca to serve our member-owners in the best manner possible.

The anniversary book committee includes (pictured left to right): Marketing Division Manager Doug Hughes, General Manager Syd Briggs, Line Foreman John Iverson, Executive Assistant Debbie Eby, Communications Specialist Randy Sobrack, Finance Division Manager Dave Lundberg, and Operations Division Manager Kim Huxford.

In closing, special contributors include the *Blooming Prairie Times*, *Owatonna People's Press*, Steele County Historical Society, and Waseca County Historical Society, along with the members and employees who have submitted photos, stories, and nostalgia. Your input and contributions have been vital in telling the Steele-Waseca story. ▓

1

Rural Life Before Electricity

Even though nearly 90 percent of urban residents had electricity in the early 1930s, only around 10 percent of rural residents in the nation had the same luxury. Private utility companies, who supplied electric power to most of the nation's consumers, argued it was too expensive to string electric lines to isolated rural farmsteads. They added that most farmers were too poor to be able to afford electricity.

The feasibility of electrifying rural homes had been proven in 1926, when the University of Minnesota, the U.S. Department of Agriculture, and Northern States Power Company started a research project in 1923 near Red Wing to determine "whether electric service at reasonable rates could be used on Minnesota farms." Known as the Red Wing Project, this effort was the first to test the concept of rural electrification in practice. Its success paved the way for the formation of rural electric cooperatives across the country.

Edith Hosfield, the daughter of Mr. and Mrs. Gordon Hosfield of Medford, in an essay published in the October 1955 *Sparks*, reflected on life for farmers before electricity.

First take a woman's point of view. Morning found her up early starting the old wood stove, so that the rest of the family would be warm when they got up. Of course, there was much stumbling in the dark to find the kerosene lamp and then there was the problem of lighting it. They were terribly dangerous and many people were burned from explosions caused by them and when they were lit they didn't give much light.

Mealtime offered many problems to the woman. Her cooking was done on an uncomfortably hot, and inefficient wood stove. Many times she found her food spoiled from lack of cold storage. It was almost impossible to keep milk on hand. It was extra work running back and forth getting food from either the basement or well.

Dishwashing was a long job. The water had to be carried in from the pump outside. Many trips a day were made carrying water.

Then there was the problem of heating cold, hard water. And after the dishes were washed, the water had to be carried out again.

Washing of clothes was a long and tedious job. Scrubbing clothes on a scrub board was hard on the housewife – and on the clothes. Later gasoline washing machines were used; these were dangerous and they had to be watched all the time. Cleaning the house was done with a broom and dust pan or a carpet sweeper. Feather dusters moved the dust from one place to another but seldom got it out of the house. It was impossible to get the house very clean.

Late afternoon found the housewife cleaning the chimneys of the lamps. These had to be cleaned every night.

A man's day also involved a lot of extra work. Early in the morning the farmer went outside with a kerosene lantern to milk the

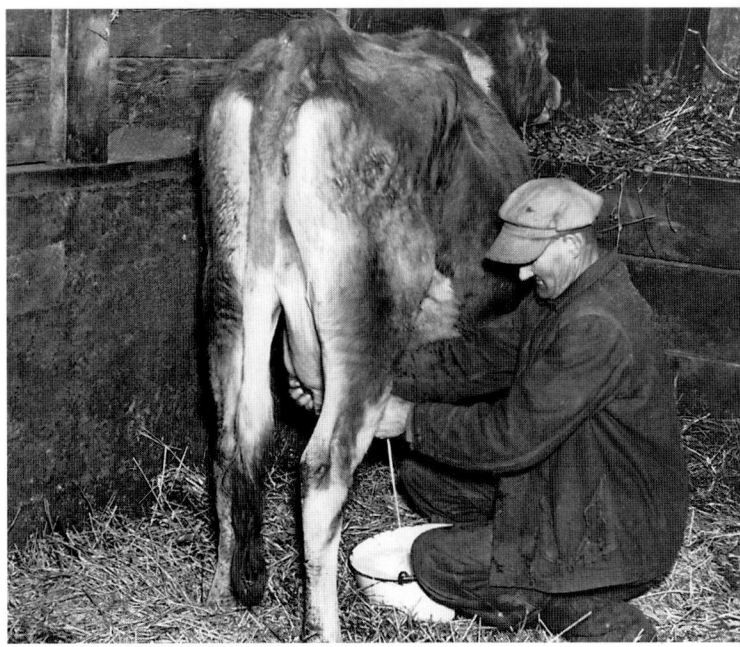

Edith Hosfield. (*SWCE* Sparks *newsletter, October 1955.*)

OPPOSITE PAGE: (*Reprinted with permission. Copyright NRECA.*)

Farmers would use the milk by separating the cream and prepare it for sale at their neighborhood creamery. Excess milk was often mixed with grain and fed to the pigs. (*Photo courtesy of the Farm Security Administration.*)

cows. This milking was done by hand and it was a slow process.

After breakfast, the barn was cleaned. This job took about two hours of work. Hauling the feed required much time, as the farmer had to wait until it was mixed. This mixing was done by hand without any electricity.

Don Resler, retired director and former president of the Steele-Waseca Cooperative Electric Board of Directors, recalled being a teenager coming in from "haying" with horses in the early summer and being hot, sweaty, itchy, and dirty from the work with no way to heat a large volume of hot water for a shower or bath. So, they would "wash up" in the stock tank after the horses drank. After they got power and an electric water heater, he has been thankful every day for hot water and he "never complained" about an electric bill when he thought about how much "fun" it was using the stock tank.

John Lienke of rural Pemberton recalled growing up taking a bath once a month in a thirty-gallon galvanized tub. He also recalled how they would milk the cows and separate the cream, where it would go to the creamery in Alma City. Coal was used and he hauled coal from Waldorf in his Model T at a cost of $9 per ton. If he shoveled it from the railroad car it was a dollar a ton cheaper.

The Franklin D. Roosevelt administration believed if private enterprise could not supply electric power to the people, then it was the duty of the government to do so. With the uneven progress of industry and agriculture, an opening came with the Emergency Relief Act of 1935. The problem of unemployment was prevalent and the position of agriculture and industry impaired. Rural electrification offered projects that would provide jobs, stimulate manufacturing, and aid the farmer.

Accordingly, Congress appropriated funds and President Roosevelt, by an executive order dated

The Old Way of Taking a Bath—Glen Bendorf

(*SWCE* Sparks *newsletter, February 1947.*)

President Franklin D. Roosevelt. (*Photo courtesy of the Library of Congress.*)

May 11, 1935, created the Rural Electrification Administration (REA). A year later, Congress passed the Norris-Rayburn Act, which was a ten-year integrated program for electrifying American farms and authorized appropriations of $410 million.

In essence, the REA was a financing agency charged with responsibility for a long-term plan that consisted of allocating funds for the construction of rural lines. These funds were not grants, but loans made to private companies, to public agencies, or to cooperatives, to be repaid within twenty-five years with interest.

According to REA Administrator Morris L. Cooke, in his article "Electrifying the Countryside," when the REA plan was outlined, farmers learned that tenants as well as landlords could secure electric power and that, as security for the government loan, a lien was placed on the government financed power line and its revenues, not on the farmer's property. They learned money allocated for building a line covered its entire cost, including a service line to each farmhouse served; a cooperative group must be incorporated; and a project must be deemed self-liquidating by the REA to secure a loan.

Many groups opposed the federal government's involvement in developing and distributing electric power. This was especially true of utility companies, who believed the government was unfairly competing with private enterprise.

The impact of this successful effort would be reflected upon several years later by Arlene Schmeling, the daughter of Mr. and Mrs. Arthur Schmeling of Hayfield, in an essay published in the July 1954 *Sparks* newsletter, which nicely reflected the advancements allowed with the creation of the REA:

Electric power has become more than a matter of convenience and proved its dollar and cents value to the farmer of today. The real value of electricity is shown outside the farmhouse.

The 'dark ages' farmer, upon rising, kindled the fire in the kitchen range, lit the lantern and went to the barn where he started the task of milking a herd of cows by hand. The milk separator was probably powered by a gasoline engine or, in most cases, turned by hand. He

> **Today's farmer, as my dad, can accommodate a herd of cows two or three times larger because his electric milker is ready for use at the turn of a switch.**

cleaned the barn with his dependable fork, pumped water with the aid of a windmill, a gasoline engine, or by hand. Tractor or a stationary gasoline engine were used where the farmer needed belt power. Winter added drudgery to the daily chores. The farmer's back had to bear much of the burden now done by electric power. This, alone, was ample reason for rural boys and girls leaving the farm.

Today's farmer, as my dad, can accommodate a herd of cows two or three times larger because his electric milker is ready for use at the turn of a switch. The milk and milk utensils are kept clean, sterilized, and cool by his electric helper. The barn may be equipped with an electrically powered gutter cleaner. The jet pump automatically provides water piped to any part of the farmstead, where it may be used for cattle, horses, sheep, hogs, and poultry. Litters of pigs may be produced in any weather by using electric brooders to keep little pigs warm and away from their mother where they might be crushed. Chicks may be brooded by an electric hen. Better egg production is obtained by providing longer days by artificial light. These eggs may be cooled, graded, and stored by electricity. At any season, electricity is indispensable when the farmer may use the power for filling silo and haymow, drying hay, grinding feed, cutting wood, welding, sharpening tools, drilling, soldering, sawing, mowing lawn, filling corn or grain bins.

Electricity is the farmer's most efficient and economical hired hand. Willie the Wiredhand asks for no time off, never oversleeps, and will tackle any job.

The wife of the 'dark ages' farmer had to care for a messy coal or wood heater and range. Water had to be carried from the pump for washing, cleaning, and drinking. The basement was the only place that could be used to cool and store foods in the summer.

Today, electrically equipped farm houses mean the rural family is given equal footing with his city cousin. The home may have all the comforts of a city home with electrical helpers ready to lighten the work of the farmer and his family. The farmer's wife and daughters have appliances at their disposal in every room. The home may be heated and air conditioned by the use of electricity and water is heated and pumped throughout the house by the same helper. Cooking by electricity is speedy and clean, and food is stored in a refrigerator or freezer to prevent spoilage. Ironing, sewing, washing, and cleaning are less tiresome when electricity pitches in to help.

Now, after a day's work shortened by electric power, the farm family may be entertained by television or radio made possible only by electricity. Any pastime is made more enjoyable by eye-saving electric light. Disruption of current in times of inclement weather situations helps us realize how dependent and pampered we are with the service of our competent Steele-Waseca Cooperative Electric. Although dad has fumed when he has had to wait for the linemen to make the necessary repairs on the circuit, he knows that the accommodation he receives from these same dependable workers leaves nothing to be desired. The letters, REA could also stand for Rapid, Efficient Accommodation.

Willie Wiredhand was created in 1950 and used by cooperatives to promote the use of electricity. (*SWCE* Sparks *newsletter, May 1954.*)

WHAT ONE KILOWATT HOUR MEANS

TO THE FARM HOME

LIGHTING FOR A WHOLE EVENING'S READING

CORRECT TIME FOR THREE WEEKS

PUMPS ALL THE WATER WANTED FOR TWO DAYS

TWO HOURS OF EASY IRONING

TWO THOROUGH HOUSE CLEANINGS

RUNS A SEWING MACHINE TWO MONTHS WITH AVERAGE USE

PRESERVES THE AVERAGE FAMILY'S FOOD FOR 15 HOURS

ONE LARGE WEEKLY WASH

(Photos reprinted with permission. Copyright NRECA.)

In REA, as in other cases, the business is no better than the people who operate it. The Steele-Waseca Cooperative Electric owes much to the former manager and Mr. Howard McKee, the present manager, along with his directors, competent secretaries, and capable linemen and repairmen.

Our everyday living teems with the blessings of electricity. We rural students attend schools which have been made more attractive, and hospitals and health centers for the benefit of the whole community have saved lives with equipment in common use because of the miracles of electricity.

Electricity has made our community a place where there are more things to enjoy and more time to enjoy them. ▪

2

Starting the Cooperative

Locally, the seed that grew into a network of REA lines serving thousands of farmers was planted on October 5, 1935, at a meeting of the Havana Farm Bureau. According to the February 10, 1938, *Blooming Prairie Times*, Alex Chambers, Barney Nicklawske, and Edward Springer had heard of the approval in Washington of an allotment for rural electrification and had separately been considering the possibility of a unit for Steele County.

Former Steele-Waseca Director of Operations Eugene "Nick" Nicklawske, whose father began the effort to start up the co-op, reflected on his father's experience, "The idea was started by a trip to the Waterloo Dairy Congress Fall of 1934 where there was a booth explaining the REA Program. Dad came home with a bunch of folders and made contact with G. A. Strobel, the County

agent in Steele County. Alex Chambers a neighbor joined with them and Steele Counties part was on the way."

Barney Nicklawske and Chambers spoke to the Havana Farm Bureau regarding the idea. A committee of three was appointed to investigate the feasibility. At a later meeting in Havana, J. H. Hay, deputy agricultural commissioner, presented general information regarding the federal REA plan. Following the meeting, Chambers, Springer, and Nicklawske visited County Agent G. A. Strobel to obtain his counsel on the project. A series of meetings were planned in the county to explain the REA loan to farmers and the general setup under which a project would operate.

A joint meeting with representatives of Claremont and Merton, Havana, Aurora, and Owatonna townships heard Hay explain how the project would have to be a countywide effort in order to secure federal aid. As a result of the informational session, a committee was formed with three men representing each township.

January 28, 1936, was the day on which the new Steele project would blossom into a full-fledged undertaking. Over seven hundred farmers attended a meeting held in the courtroom of the Steele County Courthouse. Many were turned away due to the lack of space to accommodate them. There was near unanimous interest for a Steele County organization to promote farmstead wiring and fourteen directors were appointed. The directors elected Alex Chambers, chairman; Barney Nicklawske, vice-chairman; and Edward Springer, secretary-treasurer. The organization was named Steele County Cooperative Electric.

Meanwhile, in Waseca County efforts were in motion to form their own organization. A group of farmers, particularly in the southern half of Waseca County, became interested in the possibilities of getting electricity on their farms after passage of the act which created the REA in Washington. Since there were a number of farmers being served by high-lines in and around Waseca, the first countywide REA meeting was held at New Richland on December 20, 1935.

The *Blooming Prairie Times* reported at this meeting Mr. Barnhill, supervising engineer from Washington, D.C., and Mr. Rosetter of the State Department of Agriculture, explained the proposition, and it was decided to form a temporary rural electrification organization. The temporary officers elected included: Frank H. Johnson, New Richland, president; Chris Shurson, New Richland, vice president; and Arvid Sponberg, New Richland, secretary.

The temporary officers subsequently called a countywide meeting at Waseca with J. H. Hay, who discussed the articles of incorporation and the REA plan. At this meeting, the articles were adopted, published, and filed. They designated February 15, 1936, as the date of the commencement of the organization. The capital stock of the company was set at $3,500 divided into 1,750 shares at $2 each. The articles provided the company may commence business when 20 percent of the stock had been sold. Each stockholder would be restricted to one share.

The first permanent officers elected in Waseca County, a director from each township, included: Frank Johnson, president; A. A. Lynch, vice president; Arvid Sponberg, secretary-treasurer; and the directors: Sterling Hawkes, Woodville; Ed Rosenthal, Iosco; J. J. Cahill, Janesville; Eugene Glynn, Alton; Stuart Root, Byron; Wm. Hasher, Freedom; Herman Vogelsang, Vivian; Chas. McCoy, Wilton; and J. B. Lee, Blooming Grove.

Solicitors were appointed in each township and a canvass was made in the territory. Preliminary maps were drawn up and sent to Washington and were approved. The number of customers

OPPOSITE PAGE: The original directors of Steele County Cooperative Electric include (top row, left to right): William Paulson, Lemond; Edward Springer, Merton; Alex Chambers, Havana; Barney Nicklawske, at large; Alois Wencl, Blooming Prairie; Arthur B. Johnson, Berlin; John Karaus, Meriden; Peter Nelson, Owatonna. Bottom row (L-R): Edward Ebenhoh, Claremont; Sam Prestegard, Aurora; Charles Calverly, Summit; Allan Kasper, Somerset; and County Agent G. A. Strobel. Not pictured: George Brady, Deerfield and Percy Gilman, Medford. (Blooming Prairie Times, *February 10, 1938*.)

secured averaged 2.8 per mile and approximately 300 miles of line were mapped out. As soon as the temporary plans were approved in Washington, an effort was made to secure a power contract with existing power companies, but a suitable rate could not be secured.

In Steele County, the next task was organizing each township. Havana and Ellendale exhibited "leadership in enthusiasm." The committee began the work of signing after a meeting in Ellendale. "Other township meetings were held in Aurora, Meriden, Merton, [sic] Owatonna, Medford, Lemond, Blooming Prairie, and at the Rice Lake church for Claremont, Clinton Falls, Somerset, Summit and Deerfield."

Working with the directors was County Agent G. A. Strobel, who played an important part during the entire organization of the project. He and the directors were busy holding meetings, "encouraging committee members and aiding with the signing."

"At that time the economy was so bad, they didn't even have two bucks to pay the membership."

Signing was slow at first. The "Electric" voted to incorporate and then pushed the roundup for members. It was hard to sell the idea to people, as few believed the government would advance the money.

"At that time the economy was so bad, they didn't even have two bucks to pay the membership," recalled Don Resler, as his father, Anton, rode with Director Ed Springer during the membership drive.

By June 1, 250 were signed up "and an intensive drive was started to fill the gaps in the line. By July 3, when the application was sent to Washington there were 434 cooperators. A map of the projected route, 185 miles long to be built at a cost of $185,000 was forwarded to REA headquarters."

The next hurdle was securing a wholesale power rate acceptable to Washington. The county-wide project was too large for Owatonna Municipal Utilities to handle without the addition of equipment. "Later the directors contacted Northern States Power company, Interstate Power company and the Austin Municipal plant." According to the *Blooming Prairie Times*, "The project seemed doomed at that point, for without an acceptable power rate, the federal loan would not be issued."

Strobel, Nicklawske, and Chambers considered a plan of building a power plant as part of the project and locating it at Ellendale. The plan was to serve Steele, Waseca, and Freeborn counties. A tri-county meeting was held at Ellendale and attended by representatives from Steele, Waseca, and Freeborn. The proposition was thoroughly discussed, a plan outlined, and a second meeting scheduled for the following week. Steele and Waseca counties were enthusiastic over the idea, but Freeborn decided not to commit to the plan after giving it further consideration. Mr. Zinder with the Rural Electrification Administration's rate department said he would see that a rate was made that day or he would recommend the construction of the Ellendale plant on a government loan.

A rate was agreed upon, the first to be secured from a utility in the state of Minnesota. The board president and secretary would sign the wholesale power contracts with Interstate Power Company of Albert Lea on November 17, 1936. However, prior to that time, the Steele and Waseca "Electrics" were still two separate organizations and REA officials in Washington advised the two groups join together.

On September 1, 1936, the merger of the two units was announced and a federal allotment of $275,000 was approved two days later and would cover 281 miles of line. The northern half of Waseca County was cut from the project as subscribers were too scattered and additional signers could not be secured in a reasonable length of time. The stockholders of Waseca Cooperative Electric and Steele County Cooperative Electric voted to consolidate on October 10, 1936. The new association formed by "re-incorporating" was named Steele-Waseca Cooperative Electric.

Steele members wanted the cooperative's office to be located in Owatonna. Waseca members demanded it be located there with the offering of free space in the community building in Waseca. In the end a compromise was reached with the REA office located in Waseca and five of the nine directors awarded to Steele. Officers of Steele-Waseca were: Arvid Sponberg, New Richland, president; Arthur B. Johnson, New Richland, vice president; Edward Springer, Owatonna, secretary-treasurer. Directors included: Alex Chambers, Havana; Allan Kasper, Somerset; Stewart Root, Waseca; A. A. Lynch, Waseca; Barney Nicklawske, Havana; and Frank Johnson, New Richland. L. P. Zimmerman, who worked with the effort in Waseca County, was chosen manager. The paid membership at that time was 860—426 from Waseca County and 434 from Steele County. On December 24, 1936, Chris Shurson of New Richland was appointed to fill the vacancy from Frank Johnson resigning.

Zimmerman stated this was the first project in Minnesota to make satisfactory agreements with power companies for the furnishing of "juice" for their lines. The poles carried two three-phase lines, which would have a capacity large enough to take care of a 50 percent increase in customers along the lines and additional two-phase and single-phase lines.

Board President Arvid Sponberg died May 23, 1937, due to an accidental death by asphyxiation from carbon monoxide gas. He was succeeded by Board Vice President Arthur B. Johnson. Edward V. Doyle was appointed to the board on June 1, 1937. (Blooming Prairie Times, *February 10, 1938.*)

Steele-Waseca Cooperative Electric would soon be growing. According to the *Blooming Prairie Times*, the Rice County REA was first discussed in late December 1935 at a meeting held in the Northfield Community Building and sponsored by the Tri-County Co-operative Oil Company. Steps were taken to organize the cooperative in January 1936 at a meeting in the Northfield Community Building. At that time, Cannon Valley Co-Operative Power and Light Association was selected, bylaws were made, and the following officers selected: J. T. Holmes, president; George H. Miller, vice president; Donald Sommers, secretary;

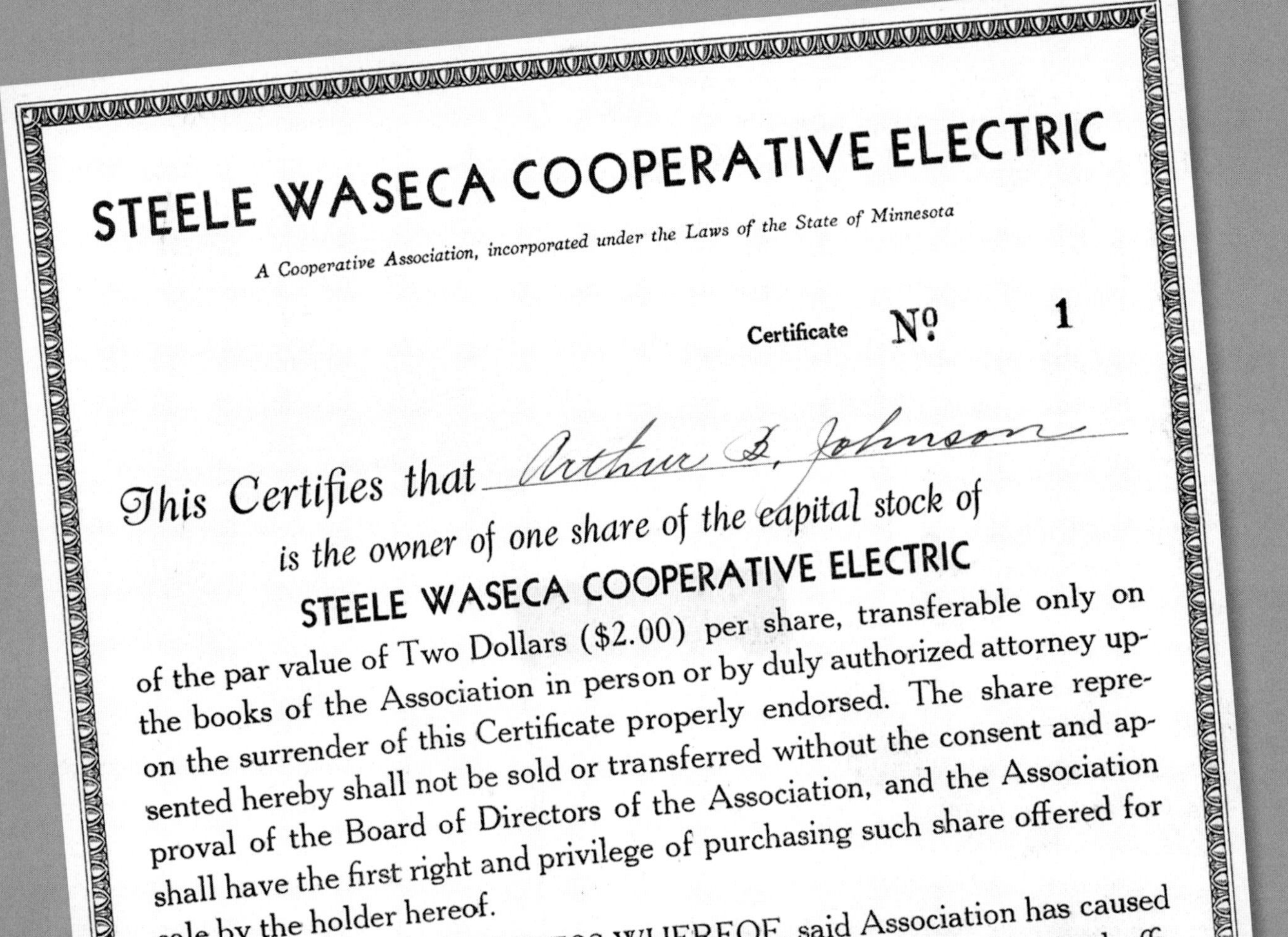

STEELE WASECA COOPERATIVE ELECTRIC

A Cooperative Association, incorporated under the Laws of the State of Minnesota

Certificate N⁰ 1

This Certifies that _Arthur B. Johnson_
is the owner of one share of the capital stock of
STEELE WASECA COOPERATIVE ELECTRIC
of the par value of Two Dollars ($2.00) per share, transferable only on the books of the Association in person or by duly authorized attorney upon the surrender of this Certificate properly endorsed. The share represented hereby shall not be sold or transferred without the consent and approval of the Board of Directors of the Association, and the Association shall have the first right and privilege of purchasing such share offered for sale by the holder hereof.

IN WITNESS WHEREOF, said Association has caused this Certificate to be signed by its duly authorized officers and its corporate seal to be hereunto affixed this 2nd day of December, 1936.

(SEAL)

PRESIDENT.

SECRETARY.

Shares Each

$2.00

The first membership certificate for Steele-Waseca Cooperative Electric was issued to Arthur B. Johnson in 1936.

and Chas. H. Wallace, treasurer. A loan was received from the Rice County Farm Bureau to aid in the organizing work.

Shortly afterward a countywide meeting was held at Ochs Hall in Faribault and interest ran high. A chairman was named for each township whose duty it was to supervise and organize his township. With their efforts and those of Secretary Sommers and County Agent Don Marti, the project was guided to eventual success. Rice County was also experiencing problems with obtaining a low power rate. When they learned Steele-Waseca had secured a good power rate and their federal allotment, a meeting was arranged with Sommers, Marti, and Steele-Waseca Project Manager Louis P. Zimmerman with getting power from Steele-Waseca which resulted in a proposition of merger. The vote to merge came at a Cannon Valley stockholders' meeting on March 2, 1937. After the Steele-Waseca Board of Directors approved the merger on March 3, 1937, the REA administration in Washington approved the merger, which added another 443 members to the cooperative's membership.

Work on the first major contract began in June 1937 with an initial crew of 150 men. Zimmerman estimated approximately $400,000 would be invested in the project before completion. An average of five hundred feet of lead-in wire was needed for each farm in addition to meters and

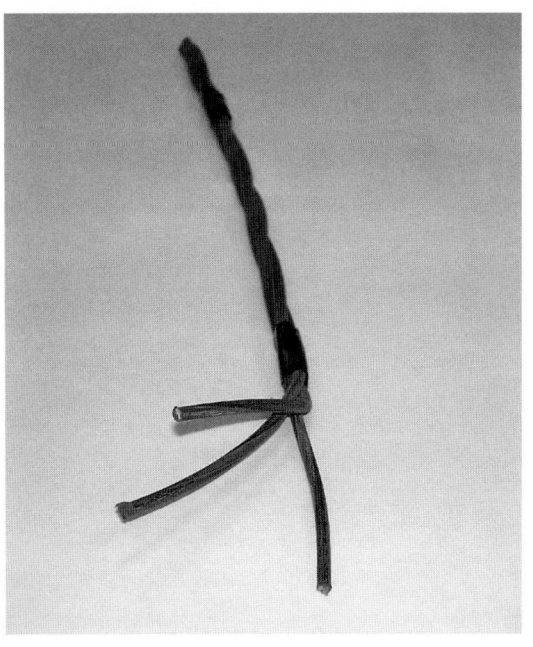

Pictured is wiring used for the original lines of Steele-Waseca's system. According to Line Foreman John Iverson, much of this wiring was retired after the 1991 Halloween storm due to breakage from the ice. (*Photo by Randy Sobrack.*)

other pertinent equipment. He stated the average farmer invested between $250 and $300 for wiring their farmstead. Zimmerman told of the problems of securing right-of-ways and easements without the power of public domain and condemnation proceedings, but public opinion and pressure from neighbors served practically as well. It was necessary to secure over seven hundred easements for this project, which involved considerable time and effort. Zimmerman commended County Agent G. A. Strobel for his untiring efforts, those of the Waseca County agent, and efforts by members of the board of directors for much of the success of the project.

The project involved considerable bookkeeping and business management. There would be taxes, insurance maintenance, and other expenses in addition to the job of retiring the twenty-year term loan from the government received at the interest rate of 2.7 percent. Among the customers, which averaged nearly three per line of high-line, were fourteen cooperative creameries. This was part of a ten-year federal government program in which $50 million was allotted and expended from May 1936 to July 1, 1937. Zimmerman reported over $3.25 million was being spent on REA work in Minnesota.

Potential uses for electricity on the farm far exceeded the average use made of it by urban consumers. Bearing this in mind, rates were set to give farmers cheap electricity in order that

(SWCE file photo.)

they might enjoy its full benefits. The patron that used only the minimum of 40 kilowatt-hours paid a comparatively high rate of $0.10 per kilowatt-hour. However, the patron who really benefited the most, and enjoyed a cheap rate, was the one who smartly used enough electricity to get into the cheaper rates. That patron received from five to ten times as much use from his electricity, yet paid only a small amount more.

Meanwhile, the first pole for Steele-Waseca Cooperative Electric was set at Beaver Lake on July 5, 1937. "Several thousand" people gathered to watch the placing of the first pole in the initial 350-mile transmission line system of Steele-Waseca Cooperative Electric. The formal setting of the first pole took place at the Beaver Lake Park in the morning with a program of musical and dramatic features and speakers marking the afternoon. With Chief Justice Henry M. Gallagher as the principal speaker, the afternoon crowd also heard John A. Hartle of Havana, State Representative M. R. Cashman of Owatonna, State Senator G. P. Madden of Waseca (then attorney for the cooperative), and L. P. Zimmerman, co-op manager, after an initial introduction by Board President Arthur B. Johnson.

REA RATES

40 kwh or less per mo.	$4.00
80 kwh per month	$5.80
100 kwh per month	$6.30
150 kwh per month	$7.55
200 kwh per month	$8.80
250 kwh per month	$9.55
300 kwh per month	$10.30
350 kwh per month	$11.05
400 kwh per month	$11.80
500 kwh per month	$13.30

(Blooming Prairie Times, February 10, 1938.)

With all the work that had been done and all that was ahead, Steele-Waseca Cooperative Electric conducted their first annual meeting on October 15, 1937, at the Waseca Community Building. "Several hundred" were in attendance to hear membership was at 1,200, with an additional 450 centered in the Faribault and Northfield areas of Rice County joining as soon as an additional allotment was received from the REA. It was determined at the meeting that one-third of the board would be elected for three-year terms, one-third for two-year terms, and one-third for a one-year term, so a third of the board would be up for election each year. B. W. Nicklawske, Havana Township; Chris Shurson, New Richland; and Edward Doyle, Waldorf were elected to three-year terms. Alex Chambers, Havana Township; Allan Kasper, Somerset Township; and Andrew A. Lynch, Waseca were elected to two-year terms. Elected to one-year terms were Board President Arthur B. Johnson, Berlin Township; Vice President Stewart J. Root, New Richland; and Edward J. Springer, Merton Township. ■

Oriet and Roy Grunwald were pictured in 1986 displaying the flag on the pole dedicated at Beaver Lake on July 5, 1937. Roy was a lineman with Interstate Power and was given permission to climb and retrieve the flag. He would later work for Steele-Waseca.

The community building in Waseca today is the Neighborhood Service Center at 203 NW Third Avenue. (*Photo by Randy Sobrack.*)

3

Building the Service

Steele-Waseca Cooperative Electric energized their first line on February 7, 1938. At that time 182 members were billed for electric service. The work to build power lines was very physical and hard. Every pole, every anchor, was dug by hand. They used digging equipment called jobbers, banjo and spoon, and frost bar to dig holes.

According to Steele-Waseca Line Foreman John Iverson, the poles at that time were set and carried into place by hand, mostly using tools called a jib backboard and pike poles. They were set or raised into place by gradually being tipped upright, butt in the hole against the backboard and the jib supporting the lifted pole until the long pike poles could be used to stand the pole up enough that it slid into the hole upright. The pole was then straightened with the pike poles, turned the right direction with a cant hook, which is still in use today, and then aligned with a plumb bob. Soil was shoveled back in and packed with a long-handled weighted tool called a tamp. "One lazy shoveler to three ambitious tampers was the rule of thumb," wrote Iverson. Lighter hardware could be attached to the pole, called framing, on the ground. However, heavier equipment such as the transformers, switches, large strings of insulators, etc., were too heavy to attach prior to setting the pole. These were framed when the pole was set by means of a block and tackle, which was sometimes referred to as rigging.

Once poles and anchors were set and dug, the wire or highline conductor was "payed out" from the reels of wire or hand coils. A lineman would climb the pole with wires cradled in his arms and lay the conductor on the insulators. The conductor was then pulled to the proper "sag," which meant the proper tension for its size, span length, which is the distance between poles, and the air temperature at the time. Once properly strung, sagged, and "dead ended," correctly secured permanently on both ends, a lineman (or several of them) would go "down the line" climbing the poles again and use a tie wire to secure the highline conductor to the insulator on the pole.

For this tying in, the lineman would climb the pole, use one leg to hold the weight of his body as he leaned back and used both hands to tie (wrap the tie wire in a certain fashion around the conductor). Today, linemen don't climb a pole without also using a body belt around the man's waist and a nylon "scare strap" around the pole to support their body as they lean back. This allows working with both hands freely.

In those early days, the goal was to build the line as fast as possible as resources and time were in short supply. Typically, there were five to six men to a line crew. The lines were built at the time to get power to those who were set up to receive service. Unlike today where lines are parallel to roadways, the early power lines would go the shortest distance to the next farmstead.

For larger, longer lines, sometimes there would be a framing crew, a digging crew, a setting crew, and a stringing crew. It was like an assembly line procedure and was generally the most efficient way to get the most miles built. Most of the heavy construction was done in the spring, summer, and fall. However, with lines needing to get in during

Steele-Waseca's first lineman was Walter Semmann. He worked with the cooperative until the mid-1940s. (*Photo submitted by Margaret Frost.*)

OPPOSITE PAGE: (*Reprinted with permission. Copyright NRECA.*)

(*Reprinted with permission. Copyright NRECA.*)

Ferris Chladek in 2010. (*Photo by Randy Sobrack.*)

while the new one would be guided up. The old saying was you were hired for what was between your shoulders. Eugene "Nick" Nicklawske started his forty-two-plus year career with Steele-Waseca as a line construction groundman and wrote about getting hired,

the winter months and the ground becoming frozen, dynamite was used to break up the ground so the soil could be dug out with the same banjo and spoon tools. Groundman Ferris Chladek, who started with Steele-Waseca in August 1948, recalled when too much dynamite was used on a job west of Waseca. "It was a cold, cold, cold, cold, cold winter," said Chladek. Typically, a quarter to half stick of dynamite was used. A bar would be driven in the ground moistened with oil, then the dynamite would be inserted. Chladek noticed the amount of dynamite being used and a nearby house with several windows. There was a woman and a bunch of kids watching them work. Chladek ran toward the house, "Come out of the house! Get out of the windows! Get out of the windows! No!" Everyone was able to make it out safely, but "sure had a lot of glass laying inside of the house," as their time was then spent replacing windows.

Retired Line Foreman Jerry Lewison said if a transformer needed to be changed, pulleys would be utilized to send the old transformer down

I don't know if any of you remember L. P. (Zimmerman), he had a very gruff appearance and a deep voice and when he interviewed me for the job, I wasn't so sure it was the best move to make. But I was hired and started working for the Coop in the Spring of 1941. Starting wage was 40 cents per hour – no overtime and 8 hour days.

Digging holes by hand was the starting place. You were given a spoon and banjo spade. As they took you out to the job, which at that time was one way on your own time

Joe Hawkins worked at Steele-Waseca from 1939 to 1971. (*SWCE* Sparks *newsletter, August 1942.*)

no matter how far from Owatonna, the foreman would stop at the first stake and set your lunch bucket off and tell you they would pick you up down the road at 5:00.

In good digging you could average about 10 or 12 holes a day. As each of us were digging holes, a person would put a claim on the banjo and spoon [sic] that he liked best because of the size and spring in the handles. Well Joe Hawkins, who most of you knew was

Chladek concurred with the hard soil in Rice County, "Up there in Faribault were the worst digging, and anywhere north of Faribault and west of Faribault, out in that area, that's hard, hard, hard clay out there – and dry. It would take you all day long to dig one hole." For other places where the soil was sandy and wet, Chladek said it could also take a whole day to dig one pole in because the sand would keep sifting down and the pole wouldn't go down. This was remedied by taking an oil drum with

Steele-Waseca's crew in 1947 handling a shipment by rail include (standing, left to right): Bill Mork, Dean Erdman, Joe Hawkins, Chuck Cofer, Russell Dillon, Percy Giesler, and Harvey Hogate. Seated is Herb Krause. (*Submitted by Dean Erdman.*)

a small Irishman with a quick temper, had a set he liked very well. We were setting a pole one day and the hole filled in, so I grabbed Joe's banjo and proceeded to clean the hole out. Well, I pulled back on it and snapped the handle. I looked at Joe and took off running down the road and he after me. I'm sure glad he didn't catch me until he cooled off.

We soon learned which areas had the most rock or mud holes, Rice County had that honor.

the ends cut out and putting that in the hole and then get the dirt out so the pole would go down.

For many years, all of the co-op's high-line poles came by railroad. In the early days, it was at a location west of the Central Co-op filling station on North Cedar Avenue. From about the mid-1950s, the poles came on "gondola" cars west of the Manke Appliance building on West Rose Street. Many thousands of poles were hauled by Steele-Waseca line crews to the pole yard on

have semis that were self-unloaders, which freed Steele-Waseca crews from having to spend the time unloading.

The first substation on Steele-Waseca's system was Sub 1 near St. Olaf Lake in New Richland Township. Iverson explained there were very few substations at that time because they were expensive to build and couldn't be justified until the load and growth of new membership increased. On the main three-phase distribution lines leaving the substation, they used a very large conductor for that time, mainly because there wasn't a lot of load on each farm, but because the feeders were so long they needed to carry the current for such a distance. As the service grew, so did the number of substations, each identified by the order of their construction. Most of the substations were built by Steele-Waseca employees, only the last three, Subs 15, 16, and 17, were "contracted out." In some cases in the early days, Steele-Waseca

East School Street. It would typically take more than a day for a four- or five-man crew. All poles were laid in a pile to their length and class. This arrangement took a little more time to unload, but saved a lot of time when they were loaded for use. "It wasn't always the easiest work, as the poles on the bottom part of the rail car were really jammed together and hard to separate from one another after their long rail commute," wrote Line Foreman John Iverson. "It became extremely hot in summer in the bottom of the car trying to hook, separate and snake a pole out." In the late 1970s to mid-1980s, it became economically better to get poles "trucked" in by semi. Steele-Waseca crews would then unload them in the same manner as before onto pole bunkers. As years passed, the trucking company started to

Co-op Manager L. P. Zimmerman at Sub 1. (*SWCE* Sparks *newsletter, January 1945.*)

SALES STATISTICS FROM DATE OF ORGANIZATION

Year	Month	No. Members Billed	KWH Purchased	KWH Sold	Income	No. Miles Energ.	Line Loss %
1940	August --	1,375	150,600	114,954	$7,350.71	675	23.6
1940	July ----	1,364	143,400	108,528	7,149.75	675	24.3
1940	June ----	1,367	136,800	97,664	6,821.15	675	28.6
1940	May -----	1,339	121,200	91,904	6,599.60	650	24.1
1940	April ---	1,298	126,000	89,258	6,419.00	650	29.1
1940	March ---	1,273	117,000	88,124	6,362.75	650	24.6
1940	February	1,240	134,100	97,406	6,519.69	647	27.3
1940	January -	1,218	134,100	97,609	6,497.17	647	27.2
1939	December	1,145	123,600	92,920	6,054.49	640	24.8
1939	November	1,052	108,000	79,670	5,481.26	570	26.2
1939	October -	1,000	91,800	66,068	4,915.08	552	28.
1939	September	980	95,100	69,654	4,897.17	529	26.
1939	August --	968	95,400	69,459	4,857.84	505	27.1
1939	July ----	969	91,800	68,570	4,867.95	505	25.3
1939	June ----	954	92,400	63,400	4,650.57	505	31.3
1939	May -----	918	77,100	53,288	4,335.84	505	29.4
1939	April ---	821	73,000	50,227	3,956.67	505	31.3
1939	March ---	810	69,300	49,701	3,937.55	460	28.2
1939	February -	798	84,600	60,279	4,199.38	452	28.7
1939	January --	783	79,200	61,109	4,178.61	452	22.7
1938	December	612	79,800	50,213	3,605.32	400	37.
1938	November	624	63,900	43,881	3,190.56	360	31.3
1938	October -	612	55,200	40,527	3,046.41	360	26.6
1938	September	600	56,700	36,671	2,932.01	360	35.3
1938	August --	597	57,000	39,763	2,905.89	360	30.
1938	July ----	592	50,400	32,399	2,810.45	360	35.7
1938	June ----	576	47,700	30,049	2,596.28	360	37.
1938	May -----	557	38,700	44,201	4,026.81	360	
1938	April ----	335	42,000	10,929	1,744.75	340	73.7
1938	March --	190	43,200	9,673	962.61	340	77.6

Average line loss for year 1938—40.6%
Average line loss for year 1939—27.4%
Average line loss for year 1940—26.1%

SWCE 1940 Annual Report.

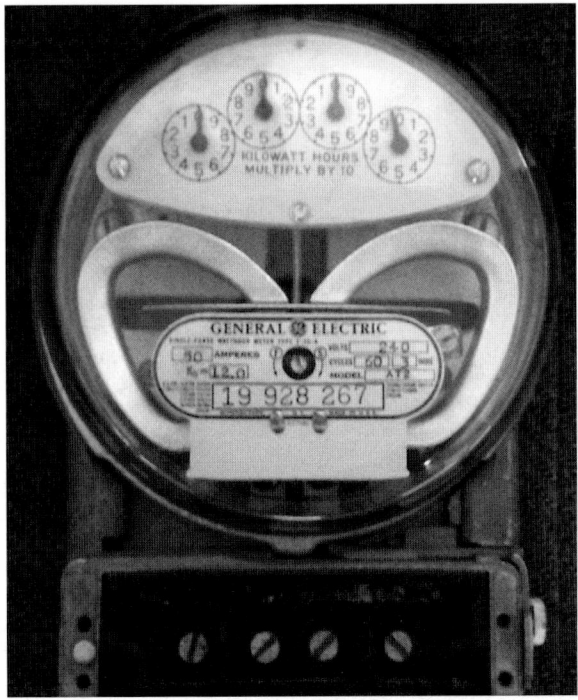

Pictured is an original General Electric meter with exposed wire connections. (*Photo by Randy Sobrack*.)

crews even built or helped build some of the transmission line to the substations.

As the electricity leaves the substation, its voltage is regulated so it can stay at a usable level as the load increases and decreases. There is also fuse protection provided by oil circuit reclosers (OCRs), which momentarily cycle power on and off very quickly in case a temporary fault such as a small animal or brush from a tree limb, and a lock out or disconnect in the event of a permanent short circuit. Once the high-line problem is located and repaired, the OCR can be reset and power flows through the power line.

Iverson reflected even though service was good and reliable for the most part, a lightning storm would take out many members because the feeders were so long. Before the days of two-way radios in the trucks, the lineman would be sent out to restore service when a member called. Some members didn't have a phone, so they walked to the neighbors and called to report an outage. Linemen always prided themselves, then as now, that they tried to restore power as quickly and safely as possible knowing a lot was riding on their actions. Many a dairy farmer waited anxiously for the power to come on so they could do their chores.

In the early days when a REA truck came into the member's yard at night checking the high-line, if the power was on, the owner would turn their yard light on and off a couple times so the lineman would know they "had juice." These were the days before the dusk to dawn security yard lights. Generally, the yard light was on the meter pole and could be controlled from the house and barn and turned off when not needed.

When outages occurred outside of business hours, members would be directed to call a lineman's home with the manager's number listed as a last resort. Outages from trees in the line were the cooperative's biggest maintenance problem. Since there wasn't communication between the service truck and office at night, when a lineman got a line repaired and re-energized, they had a designated home or farm, sometimes the directors' homes, where they could use the telephone to call the after-hours number to see if there were any more outages. Iverson explained in those days, directions were given based on landmarks such as a town hall, schoolhouse, creamery, or a well-known prominent farm in the neighborhood.

At various times it was necessary to turn off the current on some sections of the line to change damaged poles, insulators, or wire. As it was impossible to call each member by telephone, the following signals were given to alert the members of an impending outage: 1) When current would be off from 1 p.m. to 5 p.m., the farmstead lights would blink three times at 8 p.m. the evening before; 2) When current would be off from 11 p.m. to 4 a.m., the lights would blink five times at 8 p.m. the same evening; 3) When current would be off from 8 a.m. on, the lights would blink seven times on the evening before the outage would occur. This rarely happened, but at no time was the current turned off except to comply with safety rules for the linemen.

As for board representation, Donald G. Sommers was appointed and elected to replace Allan Kasper at the annual meeting on October 4, 1938; Chas. Wallace was also appointed and elected. In 1939, Albert J. Tuma would be appointed and elected to the board of directors.

The Armistice Day storm on November 11, 1940, would test Steele-Waseca's crew as high winds rode into Minnesota from the west accompanied by snow and sleet. In common with all other power and telephone companies, Steele-Waseca had some serious outages, with nearly all of them caused by trees being blown across lines. With the roads badly drifting in many places and snow making it impossible to see, it took the service crew over two nights and two days of almost continuous work to restore service.

Steele-Waseca attempted to keep their members informed with a newsletter entitled, *Sparks*. It was also used to promote the ways of utilizing electricity from features on co-op members to businesses who purchased advertising in the newsletter.

Vern Schlobohm recalled getting electricity in 1941. (*Photo by Randy Sobrack.*)

Retired Meter Department Supervisor Vern Schlobohm recalled getting electricity in 1941, "We got in the house and it [sic] was all lit up and the barn was lit. You could see every corner of the barn." Adding, "It was the most wonderful thing that had ever happened is when we got electricity. And I remember it just like it happened yesterday." He noted a refrigerator and washing machine were among their first appliances.

The first Steele-Waseca office in Owatonna was located at 342 West Bridge Street, which today is the Farm Bureau Office. (*Photo by Randy Sobrack.*)

The annual meeting conducted October 7, 1941, had a number of resolutions that would be voted on and approved by the membership. First off was the home office of Steele-Waseca Cooperative Electric. The office originally was in Waseca, but the business office was moved to Owatonna in the fall of 1938 to be more centrally located within their service territory. With voter approval, service and construction work could be handled more efficiently with the home office in Owatonna. Members also approved the date of the annual meeting be changed from early October to the first Tuesday in June since corn planting would typically be done and alfalfa hay not yet on hand. In addition, members approved the fiscal year to end on December 31 each year instead of August 31. As for changes on the board, Arnold Larson was elected over former director Edward Springer and Ed Willert of Lemond Township. ■

4

During the War

Even before the United States entered World War II with the Japanese attack of Pearl Harbor, 1941 saw Steele-Waseca adjusting to the material demands of the federal government.

With the threat of world conflict, copper, steel, and rubber were among the major commodities that went under control of the Office of Production Management of the federal government. First call for those materials went to those manufacturers who had government defense orders. Members were informed that as the months went by, it would become more difficult to purchase electrical appliances.

Following the Japanese attack, Steele-Waseca was directed by the government and REA to protect their substation "with adequate lighting, sand bags and armed guards if necessary." The War Production

Board (WPB) in accordance with their order of March 26, 1942, limited all construction to 250 feet from the existing power line to a farmstead. The ruling just about cut out new construction for the duration of the war. Among those called into military service for our country were Steele-Waseca line-men Eugene Nicklawske and Kenneth Holta. Nick-lawske ended up spending over two years as one of General Dwight D. Eisenhower's bodyguards. Holta served as a commissioned officer in the Army Signal Corps during World War II. He returned to Steele-Waseca in 1947. Other World War II veterans who worked for Steele-Waseca in later years included: Edward "Eddie" Hanson, Percy Giesler, Ferris Chladek, Dean Erdman, Leon Blaha, and Vern Schlobohm. During the war, Steele-Waseca employees purchased war bonds through the co-op's monthly payroll deduction plan.

On June 2, 1942, Steele-Waseca conducted their sixth annual meeting for the first time in Owatonna at the State Theatre at 213 North Cedar Avenue (at that time known as Cedar Street). With the theatre's capacity at around one thousand, every seat was taken with several hundred unable to get in due to no available seats. Even so, it was reported that only about one out of every four members attended the annual meeting. Prior to the start of the meeting, the Owatonna High School Band under the direction of Harry Wenger paraded through the Owatonna business district. The first four hundred members to present their tickets at the door received a 100-watt, 120-volt Mazda electric light bulb.

Among those members obtaining electricity during the war, Janet Deming of Route 4 Owatonna in 1954 described the impact of electricity on their farm:

I was quite young when we got electricity at our farm. It was back in 1942. We children always thought it was quite a thrill to go around and turn all the lights on but seemed to forget to shut them off.

There were many hazards and hardships before we got electricity. Everything we did was by hand. When today all we have to do practically is turn a switch and our work gets done. One example of a hazard was the time we had a lamp sitting on the ice box when my brother threw a pillow and knocked it on to the floor. It caught fire right away so my mother quick threw it out a door. From then on we all were very careful around a lamp.

Electricity has helped our family in many ways. About fifteen years ago it took us between three and four hours to milk fifteen cows. Now today we have twenty-one cows and it just takes an hour and they are all done. Before whenever we wanted to take a bath we had to pump water up into the attic for an hour so that it would run back down to the tub. Now today when we decide to wash or take a bath we just turn the knob and we get all the hot water we want.

According to a Steele-Waseca appliance survey at that time, a large majority of the members were milking their cows with an electric milker. The co-op was servicing ten farmer owned

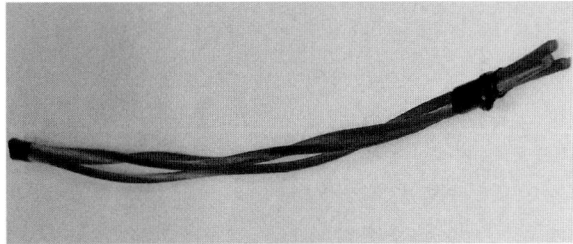

With materials not available during World War II, Steele-Waseca was among the rural cooperatives needing to use all steel wire on their lines. Lineman would struggle with its inflexibility and repairs if breaks occurred. (*Photo by Randy Sobrack.*)

OPPOSITE PAGE: (*Reprinted with permission. Copyright NRECA.*)

50 REA Members (Steele Waseca Cooperative) Bought $25,675 In War Bonds to Help Buy This Mitchell, B-25 Bomber

(*SWCE* Sparks *newsletter, April 1944.*)

and operated creameries: Forest, Moland, Merton, Rice Lake, Havana, Union, Crown, Berlin, Star, and Matawan. However, with the U.S. government placing the entire national stock of crude rubber on a basis of strictest rationing due to the reduction of rubber imports because of wartime conditions, dairy farmers were encouraged to obtain the longest possible use of their milker rubber parts.

At the end of 1942, Steele-Waseca members were being encouraged to recycle their tin cans and scrap metal. With the vast majority of tin utilized in this country coming from imports, and with those imports cut off, tin can collections nationwide were started. Steele-Waseca also made available their boom or winch truck to help farmers move or load chunks of scrap they couldn't handle themselves. To show how important farm scrap was to the American troops, a worn shovel could make four grenades, a discarded tractor could

Steele-Waseca's first annual meeting in Owatonna was held at the State Theatre. Members in attendance re-elected Donald G. Sommers, A. J. Tuma, and Chas. Wallace to the board of directors. (*SWCE* Sparks *newsletter, June 1942.*)

make 580 30-caliber machine guns, twelve mowers could make a 3-inch anti-aircraft gun, and five hay rakes could make an armored scout car.

Since moving to Owatonna in 1938, the co-op had offices in the old building formerly occupied by the Northern Natural Gas Company at 342 West Bridge Street, and had the material warehouse in one-half of a garage owned by Glenn Wilson. At a special board meeting held June 8, 1943, the board of directors voted to move the cooperative's office and warehouse to the R. W. Sanders building at 321 North Cedar Street, recently occupied by the Housengau Furniture and Appliance Company. The co-op would move to its new location on July 31, 1943. The new location provided office space, warehouse space for materials and supplies, and garage space for the co-op's service trucks all in one building and under one roof, meaning better efficiency and convenience. According to the August 1943 *Sparks*, Wr. Grunklee of Claremont was the first REA member to pay his bill in the

Steele-Waseca's former office on North Cedar today is the home of McCarthy Plumbing & Heating. (*Photo by Randy Sobrack.*)

How to "PREPARE" Tin Cans for War Duty

Clean can well and soak off label

Cut off both ends and flatten firmly

Tuck cut-off ends in can

Save in separate containers and give to an authorized collector

UNCLE SAM NEEDS YOUR TIN!

(*SWCE* Sparks *newsletter, December 1942.*)

DeAnn Kaplan.
(*Photo by Randy Sobrack*.)

"My first memory of electricity was in second grade of a country school, I was so happy to 'raise my hand' that our home had electric lights," recalled long-time Steele-Waseca employee DeAnn Kaplan about getting electricity in 1944. "I do remember my mother arguing with the electrician who wired the house. Mom wanted an outlet on each wall & the electrician said it wasn't necessary, because all the electric things we could use would be a radio & refrigerator. (Wonder what he would say if he could see homes today). The school I went to didn't get electricity until later & I remember parents bringing kerosene & gas lanterns to hang from hooks in the ceiling so we could have the 'Christmas play.' Thank goodness there was never a fire!!"

L. P. Larson and B. W Nicklawske Start on the New Sub-station, June 1944

(*SWCE* Sparks *newsletter, January 1945.*)

new office as he handed Cashier Regina Krause $5.71 for 78 kilowatt-hours used in July.

By the end of October 1943, Steele-Waseca was encouraging members with overloaded transformers during the evening hours to enhance their service by pumping their own water and doing other heavy power jobs between the hours of 8 a.m. and 6 p.m., or after 9 p.m. "Just now under war conditions it is almost impossible to replace any wire with a larger one and it is almost as hard to replace a transformer with a larger one," wrote General Manager L. P. Zimmerman in the November 1943 *Sparks* newsletter.

Steele-Waseca's eighth annual meeting was held on the D-Day invasion of June 6, 1944. The co-op tried to carry out the spirit of the day with the meeting opening and closing with prayer. Minnesota Governor Edward J. Thye was the guest speaker after the business portion of the meeting and spoke of the good work REA cooperatives were doing in bringing electric service to farmers in the state and the D-Day invasion in western Europe.

With the Steele-Waseca system growing, members in Rice County had been experiencing a lack of necessary power, especially during the peak load times from 6 p.m. to 8 p.m., so in April 1944 a contract was let for a new substation to be constructed approximately three miles north of Owatonna. In June of that year, L. P. Larson and B. W. Nicklawske drove the first stake for the new substation and laid out 3.5 miles of three-phase line necessary to connect the sub to the co-op's three-phase lines.

Due to war restrictions and labor shortages things went along rather slowly. On December 12, 1944, everything was finally in place and the new substation was "made hot." The three-phase line was "opened" at the Havana station. All lines and members north of Havana were now on Sub 2. All members in Steele County south of Havana, everyone in Waseca County, and those in Dodge County were on Sub 1.

President Franklin D. Roosevelt, whose executive order established the Rural Electrification Administration, died on April 12, 1945. His tenure in office was a continuous struggle, beginning with the Depression and ending in the midst of World War II. Although born of wealth, he fought for the rights of the common man. Roosevelt's faith in the REA and its expanding progress through cooperative enterprise was loyal and steadfast.

On August 1, 1945, electrical high-line service for the first time was available to members in the area just east of Blooming Prairie on Highway 218. The members of Westfield Township waited a long time for service as the first organizing for REA in the township was started in 1940, but due to the war, construction was postponed, and due to a shortage of manpower, the construction was further delayed.

By November 1945, Steele-Waseca had grown to just under three thousand members. With one of the biggest hindrances to quality service being tree limbs on the line, the co-op went from a crosscut hand saw to a Moll power chain saw to ease the linemen's job. With a boom on both of the big trucks, it allowed the linemen to handle large trees fairly well.

With the end of World War II, all restrictions as far as building to farms were lifted. Wiremen and wiring material were now getting to be more plentiful and allowed the cooperative to handle a number of applications for building farm services starting in the spring of 1946.

As for future conflicts, there would be future Steele-Waseca employees that served our country with honor: Jerry Nelson, Stan Larson, and Stan Eaton during the Korean War; Paul Hanson, Jerry Lewison, and John Iverson during the Vietnam War; and Jerry Mikel, U.S. Marine Corps; Ron Ramsey, U.S. Army; Gordie Schroeder and Tom Stanton, U.S. Air Force. ■

North or No. 2 Sub-station

(*SWCE* Sparks *newsletter, January 1945.*)

5

Growing the Cooperative

Another aspect of cooperative business was the billing of its members. Up until 2001, it was the member's responsibility to submit meter readings on co-op supplied meter cards.

However, billing changed in July 1945, when Steele-Waseca implemented a self-billing system where members would receive a book to record their reading for the month and determine the amount of their bill with a chart included in the book. The intent was to save paper, postage, and time for the cooperative in preparing bills for the members and mailing them out.

The first member to pay his bill under the new self-billing system was Leo Kammerer of Hope, who said, "There is nothing to it." Other comments shared by members included, "I sure like it

swell," wrote Clifford Nelson. "I don't need to wait for any meter card or any bill. Now I just get my book, make out my bill and check and everything is done." Of the 2,700 members having self-billing books, 159 correction notices were sent out after the first month, ranging from estimated bills to errors in reading their dial meters.

The evening peak by the end of 1945 climbed to the point where it was reaching the capacity of both substations. The co-op's request for additional funding on June 1, 1946, was answered by the REA's approval of $350,000. A portion of the money would be used to construct a 1,000-kilowatt substation on the Northern States 69,000-volt line about four miles north of Faribault. The substation would supply most of the members in Rice County. A second 1,000–kilowatt substation (Steele-Waseca's fourth overall sub) would be constructed on the Interstate Power Company's new 69,000-volt line about ten miles west of New Richland and would supply service for Waseca and Blue Earth counties.

Steele-Waseca's tenth annual meeting was conducted June 4, 1946, with a capacity crowd in attendance at the State Theatre. The meeting opened at 1 p.m., with two singing films followed by three selections from an Owatonna High School quartet. It was common for annual meetings to start at 1 p.m. and go for about three hours with entertainment, featured speakers, and prize drawings encircling the business portion of the meeting.

The board of directors voted unanimously March 29, 1947, to adopt a capital credits plan. The original funds for Steele-Waseca's power system were loaned to the cooperative by the federal government through the REA. The capital credits plan was a procedure to ensure every member received full credit for any amount paid in excess of the cost of serving that member. Each year, whenever the amounts received by the co-op were greater than the expenses of rendering service, the share of each patron in that excess amount would be credited to the member in their capital account. The member would be notified as to how much capital they furnished in that particular year. Eventually, when the co-op had accumulated enough funds to insure its financial stability, the board of directors would retire the equity and would begin to pay the members the capital credit equity they had earned in a year being retired. In its original format, no patronage capital furnished in a particular year could be returned to the patrons until all of the patronage capital furnished in the preceding year had been paid back. Members in attendance at the Steele-Waseca annual meeting on June 3, 1947, approved the proposed bylaw change regarding capital credits. In addition, Alois A. Wencl, who was earlier appointed, was elected to fill the vacancy caused by the death of Director Barney W. Nicklawske.

Steele-Waseca's growth from February 1938 grew from 182 connected members to 798 in one year, then to 3,904 at the end of 1948. In 1948, Steele-

Self-billing book submitted by Ron Standke.

OPPOSITE PAGE: Steele-Waseca's field crew in 1947 consisted of the following (front row, left to right): Russell Dillon, Herb Krause, Frank Mueller, Ken Holta, and Floyd Schuster. Standing (L-R): Art Schlinger, Eugene Nicklawske, Eddie Engbard, Joe Hawkins, Dean Erdman, and Dick Fleener. (*Submitted by Margaret Frost*.)

The office staff at Steele-Waseca in 1947 included (left to right): Margaret Frost, executive secretary; L. P. Zimmerman, general manager; Vern McGregor, bookkeeper; Regina Krause, stenographer/cashier; Stella Molde, stock clerk; and Mary McManee. (*Submitted by Margaret Frost*.)

MR. L. P. ZIMMERMAN

(*SWCE* Sparks *newsletter, November 1948.*)

More user-friendly cyclometers would be installed starting in the late 1940s. (*Photo by Randy Sobrack.*)

Howard L. McKee became Steele-Waseca Cooperative Electric's second general manager in January 1949. (*SWCE* Sparks *newsletter, February 1949.*)

Waseca would for the first time exceed one million kilowatt-hours of electricity purchased in a month.

After spending July at the Colonial Hospital in Rochester for treatments, Steele-Waseca's first general manager, L. P. Zimmerman, died on Friday, September 3, 1948. He became interested in the REA movement as soon as it was born. Zimmerman

was a University of Minnesota graduate in electrical engineering. He was hired by the university's extension division in 1936 to do REA educational work. When the co-op was organized, he accepted the position of project manager and would be formally hired as general manager in 1937. To those who knew him, hours meant nothing if it would further the co-op's progress. During World War II, when construction meant endless hours of paperwork, supply, and labor problems, he stayed at the job feeling that a continuing construction program was the best for all concerned.

The Steele-Waseca Board of Directors had appointed Vern McGregor as acting manager for the cooperative on July 2, 1948. Following the death of Zimmerman, they wanted to hire McGregor as the permanent replacement, but he declined the offer. The board requested the assistance of the REA for finding a new general manager and received forty-three applications.

The board of directors narrowed the applications down to three finalists: Glenn Bergland, Howard McKee, and Les Schrupp. On January 24, 1949, Howard L. McKee was hired. He started his work in the electrical industry in Kansas. In 1940, McKee assumed the manager's position with the REA cooperative in Humboldt, Iowa, where he served for eight and one half years. He next accepted a position in Cedar Falls, Iowa, as superintendent of utilities, but applied with Steele-Waseca due to his preference to working with REA cooperatives.

Steele-Waseca's Ken Holta was in charge of keeping the radio equipment in operation. (*SWCE* Sparks *newsletter, November 1948.*)

Steele-Waseca would modernize the service to their members on September 14, 1948, with the introduction of a two-way radio system. The tower was 195-feet high and with the antenna was approximately 210 feet in height. The transmitter and receiving station was housed at the base of the tower located east of Owatonna, along East School Street, just north of Highway 14. With the installation of the radio system, it allowed the co-op to more efficiently answer the calls of the members regarding their service. Each of the four maintenance trucks was equipped with a transmitter and receiving unit.

The two-way radio was credited for shortening an outage on October 10, 1949, after transmission lines from both of the co-op's utility suppliers were blown down. It was the belief of co-op management that without the radio twenty-four to thirty hours more would have been required to get all of the lines back into service. General Manager Howard McKee wrote, "High winds were experienced all over this state as well as adjoining states on that day but we believe it was particularly bad right in this area for readings of 100 mile gusts were recorded in Rochester …Here at the office Vern McGregor answered the phone and wrote down the location of trouble. This information he passed on to me and I in turn passed this information to the nearest repair crew. Our two-way radio really paid for itself that Monday, Monday night, Tuesday and until well after dark Tuesday."

"It has always been a degree of pride for the whole crew here to get out on a call fast," wrote former lineman Nick

THESE ATTRACTIVE LADIES ARE THE WIVES OF SOME OF OUR BOYS:
Standing: (left to right) Mrs. Herb Krause, Mrs. Joe Hawkins
Sitting: (left to right) **Mrs. Dean Erdman, Mrs. Art Schlinger, Mrs. Russel Dillon, Mrs. Gene Nicklawske, Mrs. Dick Fleener**

(*SWCE* Sparks *newsletter, January 1948.*)

OPERATING REPORT

	Members	Average Kwh Use	Total Kwh Sold
1940	1339	68.6	91,104
1941	1789	79.3	141,804
1942	1930	103.6	200,032
1943	1978	125	247,382
1944	2279	132	301,519
1945	2637	144	363,906
1946	3235	154	472,982
1947	3536	183	610,832
1948	3795	222	772,970
1949	3961	277	1,014,531
1950	4098	337	1,244,224

(*SWCE* Sparks *newsletter, July 1950.*)

Nicklawske. "Taking trouble calls over the years was a big challenge with many anxious moments especially when the calls used to come to our homes with no radio service. Our wives would sit up as long as we were out and take calls at no pay, as we would get one call done we would find a phone, call home and start all over again. The wives were mighty thankful when we got the radios and an answering service." The answering service for many years consisted of a non-employee who typically took calls out of their home from 4:30 p.m. to 7:30 a.m., seven days a week. Their only job was to handle outages since they didn't have access to any other records.

With the advancement of using two-way radio, Steele-Waseca's linemen were helped with the purchase of an "electric driven hole digger." The holes for the poles once dug by hand now could be done in about two minutes. This preceded the hydraulic digger derrick truck purchased by the co-op around the mid-1950s, referred to as "one of the most wonderful things we ever had," said Ferris Chladek, a retired truck driver and groundman for the co-op.

In 1949, the annual meeting was held at the Armory at 128 East Broadway Street. The annual meeting would be held there until a move was made to the Four Seasons Centre in 1977. After two years of construction, Steele-Waseca's southwestern territory would benefit with a new substation and eleven miles of 69,000-volt transmission line in December 1949. Energizing the new lines and moving the temporary substation eleven miles west required all of the co-op's lineman and several line crews from Steele-Waseca's energy supplier, Interstate Power Company.

"As we close out 1949 we are thinking about what line work must be done in 1950," wrote General Manager Howard McKee in the December 1949 *Sparks*. "The lines, sub-stations, etc. have been rebuilt in the last two years. Now we find that even with all of this new work your electric system will be loaded to capacity in January and February, the high months of the year. Assuming that growth will continue as it has in past years the system will be about 15 per cent overloaded in 1951." ▪

(*SWCE* Sparks *newsletter, June 1949.*)

6

1950s

The Rural Electrification Administration marked its fifteenth anniversary on May 11, 1950, with the announcement that the one-millionth mile of power line had been put into operation with 3.2 million consumers being served on REA-financed facilities.

In making the announcement, REA Administrator Claude R. Wickard said an estimated 85 percent of the nation's farms were receiving electric service compared to around 11 percent when the REA program was created on May 11, 1935.

The reliability of Steele-Waseca's lines to its members is credited to its line and service crews. General Manager Howard McKee informed the members of their duties and responsibilities in a column in the August 1950 *Sparks*:

First, we might discuss the service crews. There are four of these and each crew is made up of two men. One of the two is a first class lineman and the second is his helper. The Cooperative has four substations, so one service crew is assigned to each of these stations. On each one of these there is approximately 400 miles of line serving a few over 1000 consumers.

These service crews take care of trouble calls through the daytime in their area. They change meters and transformers as required, trim trees that are not too big a job for two men, straighten poles and a whole host of other jobs that two men can handle. These service crews are being rotated from station to station about every three months. In this manner all of the men keep familiar with the whole Cooperative area. This is particularly important during storms, vacations, etc.

In addition to the four two-men service crews, there are two line crews. Each of these crews has a foreman and the crew is made up of six to eight men. In each crew there is a truck driver, some linemen and several groundmen. While neither of these crews work in an assigned area each crew does, in effect, has two substations and a little over 800 miles of line to care for. These crews build new extensions, rebuild lines that are too small for present day loads, move lines for road widening projects and help on tree clearing.

We have another truck that is equipped with hole digging equipment and this truck works with whichever crew needs it the most on any given day. Many times, of course, two or even three hole digging outfits would be kept busy, but by careful routing fullest use is made of the one digger.

The Meter Superintendent has a pick up and keeps on the go most of the time, checking meters, making voltage surveys, helping the members on wiring problems, and helping the engineers plan for the future.

Two other men can be seen around the lines from time to time. One is the General Foreman and the other the Superintendent. They make sure plans for the work that goes on from day to day, stake lines and keep up with the detail paper work required in such an organization. These two have responsibility for the care and maintenance of all electric lines and equipment and are held responsible for the best and most continuous service possible.

Steele-Waseca has a tradition of employee safety as several of the directors met with the employees and safety engineers for an evening safety meeting in September 1951. The consecutive hours streak without a lost-time accident would extend to over 800,000 hours through November 1963. (*Photo submitted by John Iverson*.)

OPPOSITE PAGE: Land O' Lakes President and General Manager John Brandt addresses over one thousand in attendance at the Armory in Owatonna on June 6, 1950, for the annual meeting. Elmer Scheffert was elected to replace original director Stuart Root, who had sold his farm and was no longer being served by Steele-Waseca Cooperative Electric. (*Photo courtesy of Johnson Studio, Owatonna*.)

(*SWCE* Sparks *newsletter, October 1953.*)

Colleen Beal, the daughter of former General Foreman Henry "Hank" Cammock, recalled how her father would stake jobs for the line crew. "We had a Chesapeake Bay retriever at the time and the dog would help him stake. He'd put a stick in Sandy's mouth, tell her to sit, where she sat erectly, and he'd measure out the feet between the poles and put the stake in. So the dog earned her keep."

According to Ferris Chladek, if the roads were impassible, the crew walked to where the outage was. "It was late in the afternoon and got an outage call and went out there, and sure enough the transformer's dead. We got out there, took the transformer, put it on a scoop shovel and hauled it in. We changed out the transformer and got the guy's lights back on. What he do but come out with a team of horses and a bobsled on and gave us a ride back to the truck."

The board of directors also helped to minimize outages with the approval in the fall of 1950 to purchase "hot line tools" for the crew. It would make it possible for the line and service crews to change poles, insulators, crossarms, etc. without de-energizing the line. High-line wires also became obstacles to any high object that needed to be moved down the road. "Many houses, churches, machine sheds, grain bins, and other buildings have been moved through the SWCE system over the years," wrote Line Foreman John Iverson. "Before the days of aerial bucket trucks, the wires were either lifted with insulated hot sticks or de-energized, let down, and after the building was past, put back up. Sometimes the routines would go on for miles and there would be many crossings. It can be very time consuming work. Sometimes due to circumstances it was even done in the middle of the night, which added a whole new dimension to the process."

The self-billing system started in 1945 was discontinued at the end of July 1951. General Manager Howard McKee cited "...high costs, confusion, and the hundreds and hundreds of errors" as reasons for ending the system and going back to co-op issued meter cards.

As co-op membership grew and usage increased, finding available power at the lowest possible cost became the mission of General Manager Howard McKee. In 1951, Steele-Waseca

These two pictures were taken as John Schmidt, Eugene Nicklawske and Edward Hanson were changing out a crossarm damaged by lightning. This defective crossarm was on one of the main feeder lines that operates at 12,500 volts. These men made the necessary repairs without turning off the line and of course did the work with perfect safety to themselves.

(*SWCE* Sparks *newsletter, September 1951.*)

HERE'S HOW TO READ YOUR METER

Look at your meter. Does it look like the one at the left? If it does, then write the figures in the squares of the meter card exactly as they appear on the meter. See example shown below.

CYCLOMETER METER: Mark in each window below the numbers on your meter.

Does your meter dial have a face similar to the one at the left? If it does, then draw hands on meter card dial in exactly the same position as they are on the meter. Mark your card as sample shown below.

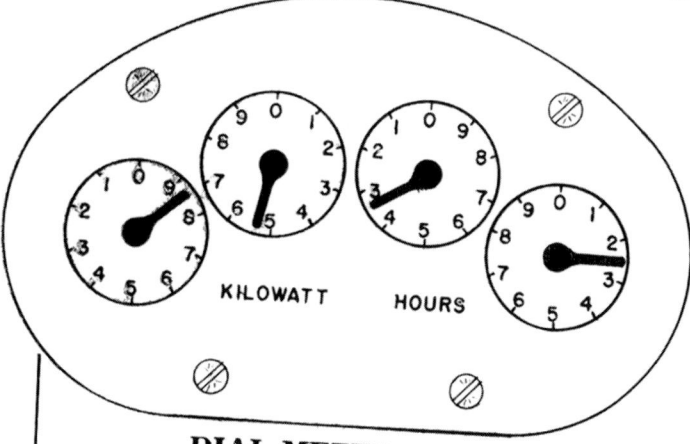

DIAL METER: Mark in each circle below the EXACT position of the hands on your meter.

In the early 1950s, Steele-Waseca's annual meetings started awarding a freezer to grand prize winners. Mr. and Mrs. Norman Loftus of Aurora Township were the lucky winners of a 12.9 cubic foot Kelvinator in 1952. (*SWCE* Sparks *newsletter, July 1952*.)

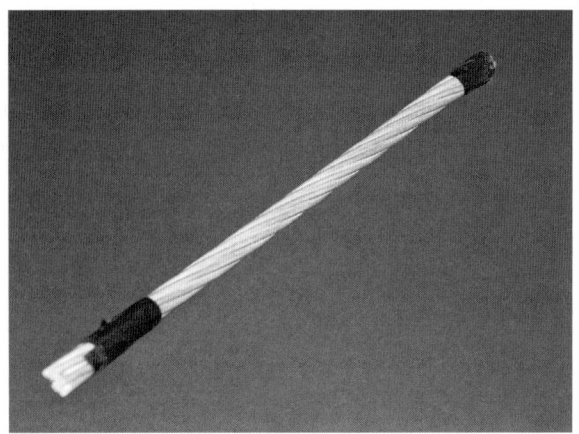

Steele-Waseca would start in the mid-1950s to utilize Aluminum Conductor Steel Reinforced (ACSR) wire for their power lines. The wire consists of seven aluminum strands around one steel strand. The wire continues to be utilized today. (*Photo by Randy Sobrack*.)

joined eighteen cooperatives in southern and western Minnesota interested in obtaining low-cost hydroelectric power from the Dakotas.

An advancement on the usage of electricity prompted Steele-Waseca to encourage members to have their wiring updated as General Manager Howard McKee noted in the August 1952 *Sparks* newsletter:

Original wiring was for lights only. It was expected that use of electricity would be but 70 to 100 Kwh per month. Now use has gone up five to 10 or even twenty times that amount. Your Co-op has spent nearly $1,000,000.00 to rebuilt lines to serve this load but not many farms have re-wired to bring their wiring up to date. We would recommend that you get your inspector to reinspect your wiring. In this manner you can be sure that there are no electrical fire hazards; that circuits are not over loaded and that circuits are fused properly, protecting against burnouts.

Secretary-Treasurer Arnold L. Larson resigned from the Steele-Waseca Board of Directors on April 25, 1953, due to ill health. Edward V. Doyle was elected by the board to assume the duties of secretary-treasurer. John A. Hartle was appointed to fill the vacancy by Larson. Hartle would subsequently be elected during the 1953 annual meeting.

Board Director Charlie Wallace would submit his resignation on August 22, 1953, due to health concerns. Jay Beal of Walcott Township in Rice County would later be appointed to fill the vacancy. Beal would subsequently be elected at the 1954 annual meeting.

The home for Steele-Waseca Cooperative Electric for over forty years was at 115 East Rose Street in Owatonna. According to General Manager Howard McKee, it was through careful planning and designing that the contracted price of the office and warehouse was $60,000 less than other buildings constructed for the same purpose during that period of time. The cost of constructing the Rose Street facility was just under $121,000. The firms that had direct responsibility in the erection of the new building were Ellerbe & Company of St. Paul, Kratochvil Construction Company of New Prague, Scheid Plumbing and Heating Company of Austin, and Kriesel Electric Company of Owatonna. Steele Waseca started conducting business from the new building at the end of January 1954 with an open house held March 19–20.

The location was walking distance for a number of employees including future general manager Don Larson, Engineer Gerald Nelson, and General Foreman Henry "Hank" Cammock. Cammock's daughter, Colleen Beal, said her family lived in a duplex next door, "steps away from work and he loved it." Over the years, Paul and Paula Hanson, Ron and Barb Ramsey, and Lois (Sorenson)

(*SWCE* Sparks *newsletter, March 1954.*)

A view of the trucks and equipment at the Rose Street facility. (*Courtesy of Dean Erdman.*)

Yule would live in that two-story duplex house. Between the house and the main building was a ten-foot walkway and a very large transmission pole with several antennas on it. One of the antennas was for the two-way radio communication with the service trucks. There was a gasoline pump for the co-op trucks in the back parking lot, which saved on having to find a filling station large enough for the trucks.

In January 1954, the co-op, through action by the board of directors, announced the establishment of two annual scholarships. Each scholarship would be for $250 and awarded to a male student and female student graduating from high school. To win the scholarship, applicants were required to write an essay on a subject selected by the cooperative. Their parent(s) or legal guardian needed to be a member of Steele-Waseca Cooperative Electric. Scholarship essays were judged by three "disinterested persons" selected by the co-op. Scholarship funds were paid to the school, college, or university when the recipients enrolled. The first scholarship awards were presented at the annual meeting in 1954. The top male and female essayists and recipients of the first scholarships were Paul Severson, the son of Mr. and Mrs. Alfred Severson of Nerstrand; and Arlene Schmeling, the daughter of Mr. and Mrs. Arthur Schmeling

Steele-Waseca General Manager Howard McKee presented the first scholarship awarded by the co-op to Arlene Schmeling of Hayfield at the annual meeting in 1954. The other recipient, Paul Severson of Nerstrand, was unable to attend the presentation. (*SWCE* Sparks *newsletter, July 1954.*)

of Hayfield. Honorable mention applicants were awarded a $25 savings bond for the first several years of the scholarship program.

Also at that meeting, members approved the establishment of nine director districts to ensure fair representation on the board of directors. The "gentleman's agreement" prior to that time was that three directors would be elected from each of the main three counties of Rice, Waseca, and Steele. The new amendment would make it mandatory that each geographic district would be represented by a director. Steele-Waseca members approved the bylaw amendment at the 1954 annual meeting by a margin of 317 to 29.

Starting with the February 1955 *Sparks*, Steele-Waseca started to dedicate a portion of the newsletter for items that individual members wanted, wished to sell, rent, or give away. Business firms needed to apply to the Steele-Waseca office for regular advertising rates. The ads section of the newsletter is among the most read in today's newsletter.

By the end of 1955, the Bureau of Reclamation had assigned blocks of power to the cooperatives and necessary transmission lines were under construction. Steele-Waseca would be among the eighteen cooperatives to be known as Cooperative Power Association (CPA). The purpose of CPA was to take delivery of the wholesale power coming from the Dakotas and ensure

Hans and Herman Hohrman performed during the 1958 annual meeting. (*SWCE* Sparks *newsletter, July 1958.*)

newsletter. The credit increased to $2 in February 1976, however the carry-over feature was eliminated. The credit today can be as much as $42, dependent on how many find their account number and if the member is on a load control program.

In 1958, Engineer Ted Ritter noted reliability of service had increased to 99.97 percent. Outages on individual transformers could be reduced with cooperation from the members in notifying the co-op when additional heavy load was being added and the proper use of fuses in the members' own entrance switch. In addition, Ritter reported numerous services were being rebuilt and individual transformers increased in size to handle the increasing loads. Vern Schlobohm, who worked at Steele-Waseca from 1952 to 1992, estimated every farm's transformer was changed out four to five times due to increased loads during his time with the co-op.

The co-op completed a seventh substation and transmission line in November 1959 for the benefit of members in the northwest portion of the co-op's service territory. Ritter reported the new 1,000-kilovolt-amp substation with a 9.5-mile, 69-kilovolt interconnecting line was located in Forest Township, northwest of Faribault. ■

the power was being delivered to the cooperatives. CPA would generally serve as the negotiating agent for the eighteen co-ops. Each of the cooperatives would retain their individual identity and authority over their own affairs.

Another incentive for members to read their *Sparks* newsletter was introduced in the September 1956 *Sparks* with the account numbers of five members published in various locations of the newsletter. Members who located their account number were directed to call the co-op office and receive a $1 credit on their electric service bill. Unclaimed credits from those who didn't find their account number would carry over to the next

Operating Report

	Members	Average Kwh Use	Total Kwh Sold	Percent System Loss
December 1947	3617	217	735,632	19.8
December 1948	3907	268	952,940	14.8
December 1949	4050	323	1,165,477	14.8
December 1950	4061	336	1,362,876	13.6
December 1951	3996	403	1,610,279	9.84
December 1952	4005	419	1,677,831	5.92
December 1953	4122	447	1,841,537	12.8
December 1954	4152	464	1,928,444	15.2
December 1955	4221	518	2,186,894	19.38
December 1956	4209	558	2,348,268	11.91
December 1957	4296	627	2,692,745	0
December 1958	4318	681	2,939,564	9.33
December 1959	4280	691	2,959,275	18.02

(*SWCE* Sparks *newsletter, February 1960.*)

7

1960s

NEW YARD LIGHTS AVAILABLE

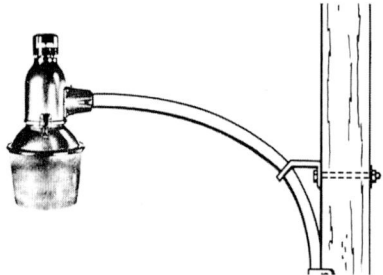

The moving of pole lines for road improvement projects had the habit of consuming a substantial amount of the cooperative's construction work each summer. In 1960, it would be no different with the construction of freeway on Interstate 35 from Faribault to State Highway 19.

As for the financial condition of Steele-Waseca in 1960, General Manager Howard McKee explained in the June 1960 *Sparks* newsletter, "Reserves are adequate for most any emergency and yet the first of this year it was possible to make a rate reduction. Should inflation not increase at too rapid a rate, it is our feeling that this rate decrease is but the first of several in the coming years."

At the end of 1960 members were invited to send their recipes in to be published in *Sparks*.

Members who submitted recipes that were published received a dollar bill from the co-op office. *Sparks* had previously printed recipes, but this was the first time those recipes were being recruited from the membership. The credit increased to $2 in 1976, to $4 in June 1980, and today is a $7 credit.

By the end of 1960, Steele-Waseca introduced a security light program to their members. For $3.50 each month, members could have installed on their yard pole a security light with a photocell that would allow the light to turn on and off automatically. The monthly fee covered the cost of installation, maintenance, bulb replacement, and electricity used. Additional costs would only apply if the light was in an unusual location that would require additional poles and wiring. At that time, Engineer Ted Ritter reported the first light was installed on the Elmer Mees farm just east of Highway 218 between Bixby and Pratt. In the first twelve months of the new program, seventy-nine security lights were installed. Even though the security light program has changed since then, today there are 2,465 members participating.

Board Director Chris Shurson submitted his resignation on May 27, 1961, after twenty-four years of service. He had sold his farm and was no longer a member of the cooperative. A. Chester Johnson of New Richland Township in Waseca County was elected at the June 6, 1961, annual meeting; Directors Eli P. Underwood and Edward V. Doyle were re-elected. Music and a magic

performance rounded out the afternoon before the fifth largest group of members in attendance at that time for an annual meeting. At the reorganizational meeting, Albert Tuma was named president, Underwood vice president, and Doyle secretary-treasurer.

With the largest annual meeting attendance since 1955, Manford Wayne of Ellendale was elected to replace the retiring Arthur B. Johnson at the annual meeting in 1962; Elmer Scheffert and John Hartle were re-elected to three-year terms. At the reorganizational meeting, Eli P. Underwood of Blooming Prairie was elected board president, A. Chester Johnson vice president, and Edward V. Doyle secretary-treasurer. General Manager Howard McKee wrote, "Donald 'Red' Blanchard easily proved to be the high-point for the day. His humorous talk kept most everyone in an uproar." Because of the extreme heat the program was pushed along and ended shortly before 4 p.m.

In the first six years of existence with the Bureau of Reclamation, the CPA saved its eighteen member cooperatives a total of $6 million in power costs. On December 20, 1963, Steele-Waseca was among seven rural electric cooperatives no longer in the "market area" of the Bureau of

ALOIS A. WENCL — DIRECTOR — RESIGNS

Louie Wencl (At Left), who had served Steele-Waseca Cooperative Electric as a director for nearly fourteen years resigned at the monthly board of directors meeting held on September 24. Louie has been bothered with rheumatism for some time.

Knowing this condition the other directors accepted his resignation with great reluctance. Louie became a director on June 3, 1947 and during his nearly fourteen years of services has always kept the best interests of the Cooperative uppermost in his mind. The directors and employees all regret Louie's decision and wish the best of everything for him in the future.

Eli. P. (Dick) Underwood (At Right) was appointed to fill the vacancy on the board of directors caused by Louie Wencl's resignation. Mr. Underwood will serve in this capacity until the next annual meeting at which time the members will elect a director for a full three year term. Dick Underwood lives on his farm which is located about a mile East of Blooming Prairie on highway 30.

(*SWCE* Sparks *newsletter, November 1960.*)

OPPOSITE PAGE: (*SWCE* Sparks *newsletter, December 1960.*)

Director Donald G. Sommers (left) presenting wrist watch to Arthur B. Johnson who retired from board of directors after 26 years of service.

(*SWCE* Sparks *newsletter, July 1962.*)

Reclamation for hydroelectric power produced by the plants along the Missouri River. Subsequently, CPA became a member of the Upper Mississippi Valley Power Pool (UMVPP). In 1965, a block of power would be purchased for the seven co-ops from Dairyland Power Cooperative of LaCrosse, Wisconsin. Then, to provide generation as required by the pool, CPA and Dairyland would build a very large efficient power plant on the Mississippi. Steele-Waseca would begin to receive power from the plant in October 1968.

Enhancements in technology were experienced at Steele-Waseca with a new billing system implemented in October 1964. Previously, six to seven office workers would prepare the bills. According to retired Office Service Representative Lois Yule, members marked their own meter cards and sent them to the co-op. Office staff tracked payments on a ledger sheet and from there the bill would be prepared. "You'd put 'em both in and they would print both at once," said Yule. "It was a good system for that time." Bills would be bundled by community and mailed. General Manager Howard McKee explained the automatic data processing with punch cards would allow some phases of the work of billing and accounting that formerly took several days could now be accomplished in a few hours. "There was a fear that it was going to cost jobs," said Gerald Mikel, who joined Steele-Waseca in April 1964 as a data processing manager. "It essentially creates more jobs because you have better, quicker information, and you can do more things with it." The new system required every member be assigned an account

The billing office back in 1954 prepared over four thousand monthly bills. The machine on the left recorded the charges and payments on each member's account sheet. The billing room also contained a mimeograph machine and addressing machine. (*SWCE* Sparks *newsletter, March 1954.*)

The snowmobile purchased by the co-op was equipped with a two-way radio, could seat two men at the same time, and pull a trailer with material. It found extensive use in the lake areas for routine jobs where roads and pathways were typically closed by drifting snow. (*SWCE* Sparks *newsletter, March 1966.*)

the co-op's southwest territory for a couple days. According to Ritter, the first crew "got stalled on Highway #30 near Kernie's Night Club for the remainder of that night and into the next day. The crew was forced to take refuge in a farm house. Early the next morning, we started two crews from Owatonna following a rotary plow to Waseca." It took about two hours to reach Waseca, but the crew was unable to proceed in any direction out of Waseca and had to remain there for the remainder of the day and night. The two members ended up getting assistance from member George Arneman of the New Richland area, who hauled a stand-by unit to re-energize the section of the line until the co-op crews could reach them.

According to Line Foreman John Iverson, Steele-Waseca at that time was trying to help the membership upgrade their service, plus add the benefit of the proper equipment to allow a farm to have a standby generator for emergency power. This was becoming more of a concern to farms that were so dependent on power to milk large dairy herds, which were common in the mid-1960s. The co-op's plan had a staking engineer meet the member on his site to go over what the co-op could do and the member's responsibility. This was a time when farmers were expanding, adding load, crop dryers, bins, fans, and livestock buildings.

Generally, the construction crew would replace the transformer pole, maybe other poles on the tap into the farm for clearance purposes. Iverson wrote:

number so the automatic system could recognize one member from another. Yule explained when a member would call in, "You'd just key in their account number and you'd have their whole file in front of you." Previously member information was on a ledger filed alphabetically. "We were the first co-op in the state of Minnesota to go to data processing," said Yule. "That took away a lot of our labor by hand."

On October 20, 1964, Steele-Waseca's ninth substation, a 2,500-kilovolt-amp distribution substation in Danville Township in Blue Earth County, began service. Members that had been served by lines out of the west side of the Matawan substation were transferred to the co-op's new substation.

A St. Patrick's Day storm in 1965 prompted Steele-Waseca the following year to purchase their first snowmobile to reach members regardless of the snow conditions. The heavy snow prevented Steele-Waseca crews from reaching the two members going through a power outage in

We'd install a larger transformer and a switch called a pole top disconnect. Member's electrician was to replace all the old weather-proof wire from the farm buildings to the transformer pole. Steele-Waseca gained a new pole and up-graded wiring which generally meant less outages, less burned out transformers, better electrical performance. The Steele-Waseca member gained all these benefits plus he now had the proper equipment to have a stand-by generator if he chose to purchase one. Everyone benefited in reliability and performance. We did literally thousands of these upgrades over the years and the vast majority are still in use today. Steele-Waseca also established a good working relationship with many area electricians. Sometimes we'd work with the same contractor 3 or 4 days a week from farm to farm.

Steele-Waseca also established a good working relationship with many area electricians. Sometimes we'd work with the same contractor 3 or 4 days a week from farm to farm.

The Steele-Waseca Board of Directors approved their first retirement of capital credit equity in December 1965. The return of $40,000 would take place with checks mailed to the affected members in December 1966. According to General Manager Howard McKee, even though the cooperative started operating in 1936, the members furnished no capital until 1941. The

board's action retired 1941 capital credits completely "and also will retire capital furnished in the years 1942 to 1949 inclusive, but will not retire capital for any member in that period whose total capital credit will be less than $700.00 after such retirement." The retirement of capital credits has been ongoing with the co-op since that time. In 2010, $400,000 in capital credit equity was retired. This brought the total amount of equity retired at the co-op to over $10.5 million.

Steele-Waseca's tenth substation would be located in Claremont Township in 1966. The co-op's engineer, Ted Ritter, reported a 69,000-volt transmission line would be built to supply the new station from Northern States Power Company's new Dodge Center-Kenyon line. Four miles of high-voltage line would be constructed by Steele-Waseca with a three-way switch so the substation could be supplied from either the Dodge Center or Kenyon end. Seven miles of new three-phase, two miles of new two-phase, and three miles of new single-phase line would be built to carry power from the new station to members. Ritter indicated more lead-time was needed for this project due to material shortages on many products as a result of the war in Vietnam. The new substation would relieve the Merton substation that had been supplying power to that area.

To enhance service reliability in 1968, 69,000-volt transmission lines belonging to Steele-Waseca, Blue Earth Nicollet Cooperative of Mankato, Northern States Power Company, and Interstate Power Company were tied together with necessary switches in order to have power come from two different sources in two different directions. McKee noted service interruptions from the

March 1966 ice storm would have been reduced by as much as a couple of days had the upgrade been available at that time.

When Engineering Aide Dean Erdman retired in April 1987, he recalled the storm on March 22, 1966. He left home Tuesday at 5 p.m. and didn't return until everyone was back on line the following Sunday evening. The storm was a combination of ice, sleet, and snow that broke over eighty co-op poles and knocked out Steele-Waseca's seven substations south of Faribault from Hayfield to Minnesota Lake. Farmers helped to dig the wire out of the ice and sleet as "Catapillers" pulled the trucks. Workers climbed icy poles to hang the wire. Erdman, who worked as a groundman, truck driver, lineman, foreman, and engineering aide during his forty years with Steele-Waseca, explained the worst conditions are at about twenty-six degrees with rain and wind. The ice builds up on the line causing it to whip up and down. He witnessed a line whip fifteen feet into the air and another fifteen feet down. Generating a terrific force, it once pulled a five-ton truck into the air that had been tied to it in an effort to stop the motion.

On July 28, 1966, Milford Rugroden of New Richland was appointed to the board of directors due to the resignation of A. Chester Johnson, who stepped down because of ill health. Rugroden would be elected by the membership during the 1967 annual meeting.

Changes in membership voting occurred in late 1968. The wife of a member could vote for her husband at previous annual meetings, but could not serve as director since she was not listed on the account. An issue came up at the 1968 annual meeting director elections, which disputed wives voting in place of their husbands if the wife was not listed on the account. Co-op Attorney John H. McLoone found the merits of the issue legitimate, which prompted the co-op to request a letter from the member if they wanted their wife to have her name on the account. The ruling not only applied for voting in place of the spouse, but would also apply to capital credits in that the wife would have to be listed on the account if she was to be entitled to the equity. Also, the annual meeting had Board Director John A. Hartle request his name be removed from the ballot. Norbert Chmelik was elected for a three-year term.

Steele-Waseca elected to streamline their billing process in July 1968 by mailing members' bills, meter card, and *Sparks* in one mailing. Previously, the bill would be mailed and then the meter card and newsletter were mailed later in the month. According to McKee, the change would save the co-op over $1,900 a year in

Board member Manford Wayne died September 28, 1967. His son, Lyle (pictured above), was appointed by the board on October 30 of that same year to fill the vacancy. He would be elected by the membership at the annual meeting in 1968.

USE OUR BANK PAYMENT PLAN

There are several banks in our area who are participating in our bank payment plan. If you have a regular checking account (dime-a-time checking accounts are not acceptable to participating banks) and are interested in a convenient method of paying your electric bill every month, we suggest that you try this plan.

In using this plan, you read your meter and send in your meter reading card every month just as you are doing. Upon receipt of your reading card the office makes up your bill, but instead of sending the bill to you on the first of the month for collection, we send it to your bank. The bank processes your bill just as if it were your personal check. Your account is charged with the amount of your bill and the paid bill is returned to you with your monthly bank statement.

To put this plan into effect, write or call at the office and request that your bill be sent to the bank for payment, giving the complete name and address of your bank. After making this arrangement with the office, notify your bank that you wish to use this payment plan.

If at any time you wish to discontinue the plan, all you have to do is notify the office that you want your bill sent directly to you. The following banks are offering this service to you:

1. Farmers State Bank, Hartland
2. First National Bank, Kilkenny
3. Northfield National Bank, Northfield
4. First National Bank, Northfield
5. First State Bank, Medford
6. First State Bank of Castle Rock, Castle Rock
7. St. Clair State Bank, St. Clair
8. The State Bank of Faribault, Faribault
9. The First National Bank, Waseca
10. The Farmers National Bank, Waseca
11. Owatonna State Bank, Owatonna
12. Security Bank & Trust Company, Owatonna
13. Security State Bank, Wells
14. Otisco State Bank, Otisco
15. State Bank of New Richland, New Richland
16. Security State Bank, Ellendale
17. Security State Bank of Claremont, Claremont

Bank payment plans at Steele-Waseca date back to 1951. This bank payment plan was promoted in the February 1968 *Sparks* newsletter. Auto pay options continue to this day at Steele-Waseca.

Steele-Waseca trucks #47 and #30 during the installation of a 69-kilovolt line in Blooming Prairie Township in November 1969. (*SWCE file photo*.)

postage. A month later, the co-op furnished the envelope for members to mail in their payments. The practice of sending an envelope with the bill continues today at Steele-Waseca.

"We tried to automate just about everything of the co-op's core business," said Mikel referring to the co-op's engineering, transportation, material handling, etc. He also noted automation was critical in the distribution of capital credits.

The faces on the board changed at the end of the decade with the resignation of Albert J. Tuma of Lonsdale on August 28, 1968, after twenty-nine years of service. Ted Skluzacek was appointed to fill the vacancy, then declared himself "ineligible" at the 1969 annual meeting, which led to the nomination and election of Robert L. Malecha of Forest Township. ■

Operating Report

129510

	Members	Average Kwh Use	Total Kwh Sold	Percent System Loss
December 1953	4122	447	1,841,537	12.8
December 1954	4152	464	1,928,444	15.2
December 1955	4221	518	2,186,894	19.38
December 1956	4209	558	2,348,268	11.91
December 1957	4296	627	2,692,745	0
December 1958	4318	681	2,939,564	9.33
December 1959	4280	691	2,959,275	18.02
December 1960	4302	681	3,110,538	18.26
December 1961	4467	696	3,468,122	13.63
December 1962	4292	808	3,590,109	9.23
December 1963	4511	796	3,954,295	11.76
December 1964	4672	846	4,010,623	15.52
December 1965	4648	863	4,077,830	10.14
December 1966	4601	886	3,945,495	9.05
December 1967	4608	856	4,820,219	15.55
December 1968	4684	1029	5,343,174	14.42
December 1969	4752	1124		4.33

(*SWCE Sparks newsletter, February 1970*.)

8

1970s

The Rural Electrification Administration recognized thirty-five years of existence on May 11, 1970, by reporting the use of electricity was doubling every five years for industrial purposes and doubling every seven years for residential use.

Applications for loan funds were exceeding what was available from Congress, which lead to the formation of the National Rural Utilities Cooperative Finance Corporation (CFC).

However, for some, electricity was still being discovered. "Growing up in the 1960s and 1970s without electricity is not only unusual but a novelty as well," wrote Darlene Zimmerman Calvert of Faribault.

I am currently in my 50s and recall vividly the experience of not having electricity. I did

not have the convenience of watching TV or flipping on a light switch.

I did know our living style was different from my class mates. I did not always like that division. When arriving home after dark we had to light a match to get the kerosene lamps lit. While milking cows we had to do so by hand since we did not have the ability to have the automatic services. Separating the milk also involved old fashioned techniques...To this day I do not take electricity for granted. We did not have a refrigerator and a little thing like having an ice cold drink still thrills me to this day.

Board Director Edward V. Doyle, who had served since June 1937, retired on November 26, 1971. The board of directors appointed Joseph R. Fox of Freedom Township in Waseca County to fill the vacancy. Fox was subsequently elected by the members in attendance at the June 5, 1972, annual meeting.

By May 1972, inflation, which was increasing the cost of materials and wages, along with the cost of wholesale power purchased by the cooperative, would increase to the point where rate increases became necessary. Steele-Waseca's practice of paying members $10 for the wiring associated with electric ranges was also being discontinued.

The era of inexpensive electricity was in the midst of coming to an end and Steele-Waseca Cooperative Electric would have to go forward with a new general manager. Howard McKee, who had served the cooperative for twenty-three years, died August 30, 1972, in New Orleans, Louisiana, where he was attending a conference for REA managers and board members.

Line Foreman John Iverson recalled McKee offered him a full-time job after vocational school graduation, knowing that Iverson would soon be subject to the draft. "I remember him saying to me, 'Go take care of your service, there will be a job here when you come back.' I will always be most thankful for the opportunity, the chance he gave me. I remember him as very serious, straight forward, polite and down to business."

The executive officers of the co-op's board of directors reconfirmed that Electrical Engineer Gerald Nelson, who had been with Steele-Waseca since 1959, would retain the position of acting manager until a new general manager would be hired. The board of directors on November 24, 1972, selected Donald B. Larson to serve as Steele-Waseca's third general manager. Board President Donald G. Sommers stated that McKee had been working with Larson since 1966 to prepare him for a general manager's position for an electric cooperative. Larson also had previous experience with Steele-Waseca in the areas of construction crews, work order preparation, warehouse, meter department, radio system operation, accounting (which included budgeting), and engineering aide.

Larson started dealing with rising wholesale rates. Steele-Waseca's power cost for 1973 was going up approximately $94,000 for the same

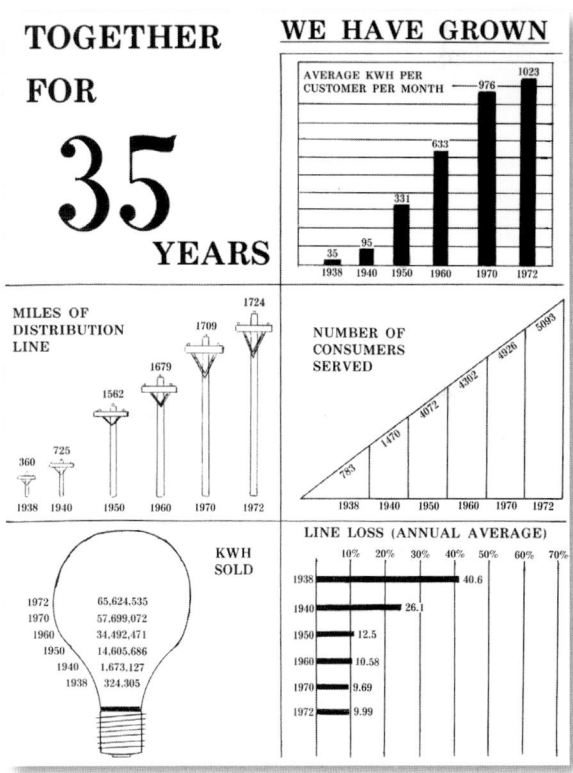

Steele-Waseca statistics presented in the 1973 *"Watts" Happening* annual meeting report for 1972.

OPPOSITE PAGE: Darlene Zimmerman pictured in March 1971. She recalled a dangerous situation with electricity in her later years, "I horrified my (then) new husband as I was about to plug in a radio as I stood in water. He couldn't believe I never knew of a risk like that." (*Photo submitted by Darlene Zimmerman Calvert.*)

Donald B. Larson. (*SWCE file photo.*)

kilowatt-hours in 1972. This prompted the co-op to start a "Purchase Power Adjustment Charge," to offset the effect of increasing power costs. Larson stated power cost adjustments would not eliminate future general rate increases, but were less expensive than filing for a rate change through the Minnesota Public Service Commission. Rate schedules were developed for single-phase and three-phase members by the end of 1974.

Complicating the issue of rising costs was the federal government's decision that as of May 1973, all rural electric co-op loan funds would come from the private money market instead of the federal budget. The REA had loaned money at a 2 percent interest rate. However, even though the REA was still the banker for rural electric co-ops, the source of those loans would be changing and come with higher interest rates.

Larson wrote in the September 1973 *Sparks* how planning for materials was becoming more

critical at the cooperative, "During the years of bounty, the era of the 1950's and through many good years of the 1960's, planning was basically simple – you knew what to expect, year in and year out. However, we are finding ourselves entering into the era of the 1970's – the end of the Vietnam War, unemployment, and as we go down the line, we are finding that there are shortages of steel, fuel, and shortages of almost every known commodity which makes planning very difficult for us at the rural electric." Electrical Engineer Jerry Nelson added, "Most of the items of hardware and so forth that used to take a few days, or weeks at the most to receive, now sometimes takes several months. Our inventory is well over twice what it was a few years ago and there seems to be no end in sight."

Board Director E. P. "Dick" Underwood resigned September 27, 1973, after moving from Steele-Waseca's service territory. The board of directors appointed Don Resler of Aurora Township where he would be elected by the co-op members at the annual meeting on June 3, 1974, to serve the remainder of the unexpired term. Incumbent Directors Elmer Scheffert, Lyle Wayne, and Norbert Chmelik were all re-elected for three-year terms.

Underground service for Steele-Waseca and other rural electric cooperatives grew during the 1970s. According to retired Line Foreman Jerry Lewison, among the first underground services was at Rice Lake State Park, east of Owatonna. The idea that distribution lines wouldn't be exposed to weather related damage and tree problems and expensive right-of-way trimming being reduced was very appealing. Lightning played a big role in causing a lot of damage to the first underground lines. However, improvements in methods and materials have made a big difference in the performance and reliability of today's underground lines.

The human factor was as much of the story as the outage itself on January 10–11, 1975. Linemen Stan Eaton and Carl Drache had responded to a call on January 10 on Highway 30 near Minnesota Lake. The wires were icing up and "jumping around." They succeeded in repairing the damage, but found themselves snowbound as they tried to make their way back. "The snow got heavier and heavier and it started blowin' and we couldn't see so we got behind a grove of trees, evergreen trees with the pickup and it stopped on us," described retired Line Foreman Carl Drache. "So we tried to get the snowmobile started. The snowmobile started but the track was froze up on it - we couldn't go any place with it." They made their way to an adjacent farm site and took refuge in a hog barn that did have power. "It was cold in there and we took a 300-watt lightbulb with us in case for heat and light because we didn't know if there was any power in there or not. And so after we got in there for awhile it got colder and colder, and so then I just kept walking back and forth for fear I didn't want to go to sleep because I probably freeze to death. So Stan, his feet got cold, so he took some hay, took his shoes off, took some hay and straw and that and covered his feet up so it would be warmer for him."

The next morning it was decided they would go back to the truck and if one of them went down, the other would keep going so someone would survive. "So we got out of the hog barn and there was a big snowdrift. We started to climb over that and Stan fell down and then he motioned to me to keep on going, but you know I came back, and got him out of there and then went to a different barn there and there was chickens in this house and it was a lot warmer in there, but we didn't know that that was there when we first got there." After warming up, Drache and Eaton would make it to their truck, where upon pulling the choke, the truck started, "The guy above us was looking over us," said Drache. The SWCE office contacted Bernard Landsteiner from the area and he would venture out on his snowmobile and find the men since there was grave concern for their safety. They would eventually meet up with a second two-man crew, Jerry Lewison and Floyd Schuster, who had also been in that area during that same storm. "We didn't know anything about Jerry and Floyd being up the road maybe a quarter of a mile," said Drache.

Lewison recalled their night being stuck in their truck as they were able to keep their diesel truck running. "We had like a foot of snow in the truck from just sifting in and I kept getting closer

February 11, 1975

Steele Waseca Cooperative Electric
Owatonna, Minn. 55060
Dear Sirs,
We would like to express our appreciation for the great service we got during the "big storm". We don't know how much we do appreciate electricity until it's gone. How helpless we are! The prompt and reliable service we got at the "end of the line" location we had was unbelievable and the concern of the repairman who even came to the house to check on us was gratifying. We've always had good service but while everyone around us was still out of electricity from other companies we were warming up and back to as close as normal as a storm will allow.
Again *thank you* to those repairmen who did the job that had to be done. Who would have changed jobs with them, then?
Mrs. Melvin Moore
R.R. 1, Mapleton, MN

February 4, 1975

Please express our thanks to the linemen for their efforts in restoring power during the January 11 storm. It is comforting to know there are people who are willing to work under such conditions for the comfort of others.
Thank you.
Sincerely,
Mr. and Mrs. B. M. Hoffman
R.R. 3, New Richland, Minn. 56072

February 3, 1975

Steele-Waseca Coop Electric
Owatonna, Minn.
A special thank you to the line repair men and those who assisted them in getting electricity restored to our farm during the snow storm January 11th.
One could hardly expect anyone to be out but yet they braved it all and got the job done as soon as they possibly could. We want you to know it was greatly appreciated.
Sincerely,
Mr. and Mrs. Geo. Dobberstein

February 4, 1975

Steele-Waseca Coop Electric
Owatonna, Minn.
We would certainly like to express our thanks to the wonderful job your linemen did through the storm of January 10. Leaving their families, and risking their lives to save and help others, they deserve to be recognized.
Mr. and Mrs. Dale Lohberger

(*Letters published in the March 1975* Sparks *newsletter.*)

to Floyd to keep warm." According to Lewison, Mrs. Maynard Schroeder of Danville Township made breakfast and they helped with the chores since her husband had a heart condition. Once Drache and Eaton met up with Lewison and Schuster, the linemen would have lunch at the Schroeders, then received a call to make their way to repair the line that fed out of the Matawan

The final annual meeting at the Owatonna Armory occurred on June 7, 1976. Retired Office Service Representative Lois Yule recalled her memories of the Armory, "Right inside the door there would be a band playing. You didn't hear the name very good. We always had a good turnout and the members had to stand outside waiting to come in to register." Plenty of free parking, adequate seating, and

1 Facilities of The Falkirk Mining Company, with the Coal Creek Generating Station in the background, in July, 1979.
Foreground, left to right: second 105 cubic yard dragline erection site, "The Prairie Rose" dragline. Center, left to right: railroad spur, 17 cubic yard dragline and loading shovel erection site, fuel farm, service building complex.

Cooperative Power Association and United Power Association.

substation (Sub 3). Lewison recalled a front loader operator of Matawan helped clear snow along the way as they repaired the line. The crew would end up staying at Director Elmer Scheffert's rural New Richland residence that night. Lewison said he and Floyd headed to Bixby on another call the following day and didn't make it home until Sunday afternoon when the Vikings and Steelers were playing in the Super Bowl.

climate control were cited by General Manager Don Larson as for the main reasons for moving the annual meeting to the Four Seasons Centre in 1977.

Steele-Waseca was among eighteen member cooperatives belonging to Cooperative Power Association (CPA) that was joining with United Power Association (UPA) to build a 1,100-megawatt power plant, Coal Creek Station, on lignite fields near Underwood, North Dakota. The power plant

Over 1,200 Steele-Waseca members and invited guests have attended the tour to learn how electricity is generated at Coal Creek Station, the process of mining coal at Falkirk Mine, and returning the land to original farmland. (*Photo by Doug Hughes*.)

and associated costs amounted to $1.2 billion. It was necessary to construct a 400,000-volt direct current (DC) power line to transmit the power. The project would eventually be completed in 1979.

The DC line would draw controversy in Minnesota from those who didn't want the line going through their property to those concerned with quality of life issues associated with a high voltage line located near them. Even though scientific studies showed the high voltage line was safe, the process eventually would become violent and destructive. Retired board member Don Resler recalled the busloads of Steele-Waseca members that traveled to the state capitol and to the protests where the DC line vandalism was taking place to show support for its construction. Coal Creek Station's Unit 1 started generating electricity in 1979; Unit 2 started in 1980. CPA operated the generating plant and owned 56 percent of it. The other 44 percent was owned by UPA of Elk River.

In 1979, Steele-Waseca would form a member advisory council. The function of the group would be to advise the board of directors and management on the needs, wants, and concerns of members by providing input on matters that relate to membership issues. The council was comprised of eighteen members, one man and one woman from each director's district. Thirty-six current and future members of the council would be the first to travel on the Coal Creek Station tour in April 1980 to Underwood, North Dakota. The tour would open to all membership the following year and has been an annual trip at Steele-Waseca since that time.

As the co-op grew, space at the Rose Street office was adjusted. The hardware, OCRs, transformers, and covered wire were moved to the co-op's "pole yard" east of Owatonna on East School Street. ■

9

1980s

In September 1980, Steele-Waseca introduced "off peak" rate structures for members using electric heat or in combination with their electric water heater.

The cost of wholesale power was causing the retail rates to increase "...due to the high inflationary construction costs of the new Coal Creek plant at Underwood, North Dakota which is supplying most of the power for our Coop and 37 other Coops throughout Minnesota." With "peak demand" typically occurring between 4 p.m. and 9 p.m., it was accounting for nearly 60 percent of the co-op's entire wholesale power bill. For every 1,000 watts decreased during peak demand, it would save the co-op at that time $11.95. To improve the cost effectiveness of electrical generation at the

Coal Creek plant, it became a priority to decrease usage during demand peaks by increasing usage during the lower demand period of 11 p.m. to 7 a.m. With programs like storage heat and the intro-duction of dual fuel in September 1981, which utilizes a conventional fuel source when electric heat is controlled during peak demand periods, decreases during peak demand times could be experienced, thus decreasing wholesale power bills for the co-op. The electric rates on both pro-grams were approximately one half of the regular residential rate. Among Steele-Waseca members,

Mr. and Mrs. Martin Ahrens of Havana Township installed the first off peak storage, and Mr. and Mrs. Art Thompson of Faribault were the first to convert their heating system to dual fuel.

Steele-Waseca would introduce metered and unmetered security lights and rates in November 1980. Members wishing to have an electrician install a switch on their security light to control monthly kilowatt-hour usage would no longer be eligible to have the security light maintained by the co-op.

According to Dale Detjen, director of member services at the time, an ice storm in March 1982 would impact several substations as he wrote,

Shortly after 6:00 PM on Friday evening, March 19, we began receiving outage calls from members in Lemond and Summit Townships. The storm intensified and at approximately 6:45 p.m., a large 69,000 Volt transmission line, owned by Interstate Power Company, lost power for 1 hour, shutting off 5 substations, #1, 3, 6, 8 and 9, which supply power to 2,465 members located south of Highway #14. Between 10:40 PM March 19 and 8:15 AM March 20, substations #6 and #8, which serve 1,144 members south of Owatonna from Ellendale to Hayfield were out of power three additional times. Two of these outages were caused by wire breaks on the Cooperative's transmission line, located along Highway #218 just south of Oak Glen Lake. Our distribution lines also received extension damage. Eight broken poles, twelve crossarms and sixty separate wire breaks resulted from ice build-up that exceeded 1 ½ inches in diameter on the lines.

By 11:58 PM Saturday night, service had been restored to all members affected by the storm and our full crew had worked 30 hours without stopping except for fuel and meals. It was a very trying experience and they all contributed to a job well done.

The following members assisted the Steele-Waseca crews during the storm: Gerth Anderson, Blooming Prairie Township; Robert Groth, Northfield Township; and Orlo Toquam, Ripley Township. Detjen added, "Without their cooperation the outages in their respective areas would have lasted even longer than they did."

As programs and services increased so would the demands on automation which prompted the introduction of an updated bill in June 1982 to better serve the business of the cooperative and informing the member of the various aspects of their bill.

Director Jay Beal, pictured above, retired after twenty-eight years of service on the board of directors. Sylvester Emge was elected by the membership in attendance at the annual meeting on June 1, 1981. (*SWCE* Sparks *newsletter, June 1981.*)

OPPOSITE PAGE: Technician Jake Jacobson (right) and Don Bos complete a satellite installation. (*SWCE file photo.*)

After forty-five years with the Steele-Waseca Board of Directors, twenty-five years as board president, Donald G. Sommers of Northfield Township in Rice County died on August 21, 1983, after suffering a stroke. Donald R. Kolb would be appointed on September 20, 1983, and would be elected by the membership at the annual meeting in 1984. (*SWCE file photo.*)

Quick-thinking trio *See article on page 2.*
Jerry Lewison, left, Ernie Johnson, center, and Carl Drache were in the right place at the right time Wednesday when they combined forces to help resuscitate 9-month-old Phillip Schleicher and get him to Owatonna City Hospital after he stopped breathing.

(*Published photo reprinted with permission from the* Owatonna People's Press, *July 20, 1984.*)

Load management at Steele-Waseca would be expanded after the board of directors on September 30, 1982, approved the installation of radio receiver control devices on participating members' electric water heaters. A $5 monthly credit was applied to participating members with at least a 52-gallon water heater capacity. A $10 credit was applied to members with a water heater in excess of 100 gallons. A further expansion was presented to the membership in mid-1985 with ground water heat pumps, which were three to four times more efficient than conventional oil or gas heating units.

District #2 Director Elmer Scheffert retired from the board at the 1983 annual meeting after serving since 1950. George Byron was elected by the membership in attendance. Incumbent Directors Lyle Wayne and Norbert Chmelik were each re-elected.

The scholarship program started in 1954 continued through 1982. In 1983, the board of directors authorized participation in the Rural Electric Youth Tour to Washington, D.C., sponsored by the

National Rural Electric Cooperative Association (NRECA). High school juniors who were dependents of Steele-Waseca members were eligible to apply by writing an essay on the subject determined by the co-op. The first two recipients were Jolene Kubista, the daughter of Mr. and Mrs. Jerome Kubista of Owatonna, and Kim Lewison, the daughter of Mr. and Mrs. William Lewison of Owatonna.

Steele-Waseca would transition from youth tours to Washington, D.C., to Minnesota Youth Energy Camps through the 1990s. Two to three youths of cooperative members would attend the camp for "hands on" opportunities to learn about electrical safety and the benefits of the cooperative way.

On July 18, 1984, Steele-Waseca Lineman Jerry Lewison was working on power lines northwest of Pontoppidan Lutheran Church on County Road 4, when Debbie Schleicher came driving down her driveway with her nine-month-old son, Phillip, in the car limp and discolored. Schleicher was trying to get her son to the hospital after he became seriously ill as a result of eating some food and going into convulsions. However, when she couldn't get out of her driveway due to the regrading of County Road 4, she frantically ran up to the line crew for assistance. Crew Chief Carl Drache summoned Lewison, who cleaned discharge from the infant's mouth and performed mouth-to-mouth resuscitation. Once Phillip started to breathe, his mother, Lewison, and Contractor Ernie Johnson used his pickup to drive them to the Owatonna Hospital. "The color changed. It was the best thing that ever happened," recalled Lewison.

The boy would recover due to Lewison's quick reactions to the situation, "You have the training [First Aid and CPR] in this, but you think it's going to happen to the other guy," said Lewison. Schleicher credited Lewison for saving her son's life, "Boy, I don't know what I would have done if he wasn't there. He just took charge and it made me feel a lot better."

At their March 1, 1985, meeting, the Steele-Waseca Board of Directors approved an assurance of payment deposit policy. For new members to the cooperative, they would be required to pay a $200 deposit. Once that member paid on time for twelve consecutive billings, their deposit was returned to them. While held, the deposit earned interest at a rate specified by Minnesota state statute. The policy became enacted as a result of uncollectible accounts. A deposit requirement remains in effect to this day.

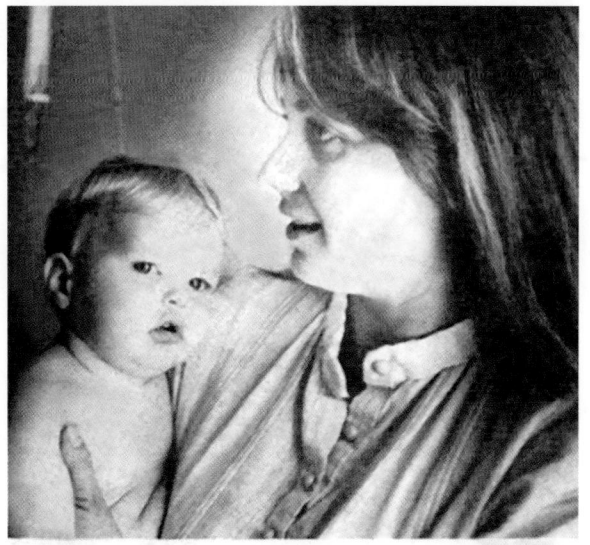

Phillip and Debbie Schleicher

(*Published photo reprinted with permission from the* Owatonna People's Press, *July 20, 1984.*)

District #3 Director Milford Rugroden retired after serving his term up to the 1985 annual meeting. Harold Amley was elected by the membership in attendance to replace him. Incumbent Directors Donald Resler and Joseph Fox were re-elected.

As farms became more electrified, a previously little-known condition had managed to grow to the point of concern in some dairy, swine farrowing, and similar operations. The term "neutral-to-earth voltage," commonly referred to as "stray voltage," described the small electric voltage existing between grounded neutral and earth on any electric system. General Manager Don Larson wrote in the November 1985 *Sparks* newsletter:

Just a few years ago the word, stray voltage, became a household word for dairy farmers. The employees of cooperatives made every effort to identify and correct this newly discovered problem. Our first efforts were hampered by a lack of instrumentation and a genuine absence of knowledge about the phenomenon. However, we were quick to learn with the aid of some fine gentlemen from the University of Minnesota, Dr. Cloud and Dr. Appleman. They shared with us techniques on how to assist our membership in finding solutions. We will always be indebted to them for their timely help.

In our first stray voltage case, Dr. Cloud worked with Steele-Waseca's personnel, local electricians, veterinarians, owners and other interested parties as he taught us how to identify and reduce stray voltage. He and Dr. Appleman were very instrumental in helping to provide a quick and educated response to our stray voltage problems. Seminars were held in various parts of our service area in an effort to involve membership and other concerned parties. We continue to monitor farms on which the stray voltage problem has been alleviated. This will enable us to act quickly if the problem should reappear. We have also provided Dr. Cloud with manpower and equipment to fully isolate known stray voltage problems on several dairy farms, resulting in the detection of their source and successful correction.

Steele-Waseca to this day continues to work with their members regarding potential stray voltage situations.

As revenue for the co-op hit a plateau in the early 1980s, Steele-Waseca explored additional revenue through satellite television service when they conducted a survey of the membership in the July 1985 *Sparks*. As a result of the membership survey, Extra Service Cooperative (ESC) debuted as its own division with a grand opening on September 27, 1985. Former General Manager Jerry Mikel, who at that time was data processing manager, said, "That was a real challenge to do retail work and installations." He added, "It's like buying a boat. The best day is when you get it and the next best day is when you get rid of it. It was sort of that way

with satellite." While the co-op would experience growth and success with the venture, it transitioned out of the satellite business in the early 1990s when Prairie Satellite of Northfield agreed to service the membership.

At Steele-Waseca's fiftieth annual meeting on June 2, 1986, Allan Kasper and his wife, Agnes, received a Pioneer Award for their service with the

TOP: Allan Kasper (right) accompanied by his wife, Agnes, received a Pioneer Award at Steele-Waseca's fiftieth annual meeting for their service with the cooperative.

BOTTOM: Roy Grunwald (right) along with his wife, Oriet, are presented with a commemorative-framed flag at the co-op's fiftieth annual meeting at the Four Seasons Centre.

Lineman Jim Wolters is pictured with a McKinley Elementary School student at an electrical safety presentation in 1988. (*SWCE file photo*.)

The format of the annual meetings changed in 1988 in response to membership surveys. A variety of food, ag, and health vendors were featured prior to a more abbreviated business portion of the annual meeting. Attendance for the annual meeting was estimated at nine hundred. (SWCE file photo.)

itself. Memberships were opened to Steele-Waseca consumer/members at the co-op's annual meeting in 1987. The group would receive a number of national awards during their existence.

While the cooperative unfortunately has had to deal with random acts of vandalism, especially insulators that have been shot causing subsequent outages, the largest crime of theft against the cooperative was discovered in February 1988 when crews found that someone had stolen forty-seven spans of neutral wire, the equivalent of about 2.5 miles of line. The incidents occurred in sections of Berlin, Summit, and Somerset townships in Steele County. On May 6, 1988, suspects allegedly involved with the theft were apprehended in Charles City, Iowa. The three Iowa men

co-op. Allan was one of the original directors of the Steele County Cooperative Electric before it merged to Steele-Waseca. Roy and Oriet Grunwald also received a commemorative-framed flag that contained the flag Roy retrieved at the Beaver Lake pole-setting ceremony on July 5, 1937. Other business included District #6 Director Norbert Chmelik retiring after serving on the board of directors since 1968. The membership in attendance elected Donald Starks for the position. Incumbents George Byron and Lyle Wayne were both re-elected for three-year terms. It also started the tradition of a meal being served at the annual meeting.

Steele-Waseca was recognized by the National Rural Electric Women's Association (NREWA) for being the first rural electric cooperative in Minnesota to set up a local chapter of the NREWA. The chapter, Steele Waseca—Women Involved in Rural Electrification (SW-WIRE), helped support legislation and educated youth on rural electrification issues and on cooperatives. The local chapter was organized in April 1986. Membership was originally limited to employees, employees' spouses, retirees, and retirees' spouses so the group could organize

LaVonne Wolters (left) and Mary Malecha led the first SW-WIRE group. The group earned PEARL (Promoting Excellence in American Rural Life) Awards from the NREWA for their efforts in membership and youth categories. (*Photo published in the SWCE Annual Report in June 1988.*)

confessed to all of the wire thefts in Steele County and either pled guilty or were convicted. Restitution of $15,851.50 was paid in full by those convicted by the end of 1993.

Steele-Waseca's Sub #14 in Walcott Township would be energized in March 1988. As the co-op continued to upgrade their system

stated the Highway 30 line was the backbone to the electric system for that area. The new line consisted of heavy-duty conductor and tall poles closely spaced together. Steele-Waseca was also involved with the reconstruction project of Highway 19 to Interstate 35 in 1989 involving extensive power line facilities, which included

In the mid to late 1980s, Steele-Waseca began to obtain large commercial and industrial loads, which added financial strength to the cooperative and eased the pressure of rate volatility. Among those being added to Steele-Waseca was Hydro-Ax of Owatonna, Viratec (now Tru-Vue) of Faribault, and increased agricultural loads like Jennie-O Turkey Store and Jerome Foods pictured in this aerial photo taken in 2010. (*Photo by Doug Hughes, CFII-MEII.*)

for delivering electricity, the board of directors at their June 1 meeting in 1989 remarked on the number of favorable comments received regarding the three-phase Highway 30 project from New Richland to the Danville substation completed by Okay Construction. Larson

co-op distribution line and Cooperative Power transmission line.

From 1970 to 1990, Steele-Waseca went from 4,810 members to 6,463. The miles of line increased from 1,704 to 1,838, and the plant kilowatts from 14,603 to 24,935. ■

10

1990s

The Steele-Waseca family mourned the death of Line Foreman Stan Eaton on September 19, 1990. At the time of the accident on September 6, the sixty-two-year-old Eaton was repairing a security yard light when the pole cracked and fell to the ground with Stan riding the side of the pole to the ground.

His working partner, Tom Lynch, immediately responded by attending to Stan and radioed the office for emergency help. Stan was transported to District One Hospital in Faribault and later air-lifted to St. Mary's Hospital in Rochester. Eaton sustained broken bones and severe internal injuries. He underwent several surgeries and there was hope he would recover. However, complications developed which led to his death.

"He was one of the most safety-minded men probably that I can remember," said retired Meter

Department Supervisor Vern Schlobohm."On that particular pole, all it had was a night light on it and there weren't any wires attached to the pole." Schlobohm noted wires connected to the pole would have prevented it from falling in the manner of which it did.

Stan was employed with Steele-Waseca for thirty-eight years, General Manager Don Larson wrote in the November 1990 *Sparks*, "Stan's life work at your Cooperative was dedicated to service. Performance of his duties was always of the highest standards." A memorial featuring a flagpole and a plaque was dedicated at the Rose Street office on May 31, 1991, with 150 people attending the dedication.

A Steele-Waseca scholarship was again awarded in 1990 through SW-WIRE. The $300 scholarship was for any member or their immediate family that was furthering their education in an electrical field. Applicants were required to write a short essay on a specified topic and submit their high school transcript having attained a "C" grade average or better. In 1992, SW-WIRE increased their scholarship to $400. In support of their scholarship, SW-WIRE would sell raffle tickets for items to be given away at the cooperative's annual meeting. When SW-WIRE expanded their membership to men and women in 1994, they became known as Steele Waseca—Volunteer Program Committee (SW-VPs). The scholarship program was continued and would expand in 1998 with at least two $500 scholarships awarded to recipients attending a two- or four-year technical school or college in any field of study.

Commercial and industrial loads continued to build for Steele-Waseca in the early 1990s. Among the loads at that time was the Medford Outlet Center, improvements at the Owatonna and Faribault airports, Northern Tool & Equipment of Faribault, IFP Foods of Faribault, and Medford Furniture and McDonalds Restaurant of Medford.

The storm that is referred as the worst storm ever endured by the cooperative occurred on Halloween 1991. The storm on Thursday, October 31 began with freezing rain and slushy snow. The Twin Cities was getting heavy, wet snows but southeastern Minnesota was being battered by the worst ice storm ever recorded as it was slowly cut off from the world. The lines began falling late Thursday night and at 1 a.m. Friday the first crews were called into work.

The family stands with the memorial plaque dedicated in Stan's honor. The plaque would be rededicated on July 22, 1994, at the co-op's present office at 2411 West Bridge Street in Owatonna. (*SWCE file photo*.)

OPPOSITE PAGE: Stan Eaton's wife, Dorothy, along with their children Michael, Bruce, and Debra, raised the flag as part of the flagpole dedication in honor of Stan. (*SWCE file photo*.)

Steele-Waseca Lineman Paul Becker at the site of the Medford Outlet Center in March 1991. (*SWCE file photo*.)

Power lines down as far as the eye could see were a common sight during the 1991 Halloween storm. (*SWCE file photo*.)

"Jim Wolters and I got called out and it was a rain sleet," recalled retired Line Foreman Jerry Lewison. "Farmers hadn't got their corn out or the beans yet." As the weather changed, "I told Jim, 'I think I'm back in Vietnam,' I hear all these branches breaking and boom, boom, you know like that."

By 2:30 a.m., the "call crew" had more outages than they could handle. "Our first location was east of Blooming Prairie," wrote John Iverson, "and as we tried to put downed wires back up, I remember hearing the sound of tree branches being ripped off the trees, and the crash of tree limbs and ice when they hit the ground. By about sunrise, it was clear that this wasn't just another storm...I will never forget arriving at a crossroads and seeing poles and wires down, like dominos, for miles as far as an eye could see."

At the height of the storm there were 3,571 members out of service. In Friday's early hours, five miles of transmission lines went down near Bixby, north of Blooming Prairie. The wind picked up in the evening. There were whiteouts on the roads and working conditions became life threatening. During the storm, Larson pulled the crews in at 9 p.m. Eight of the co-op's fourteen substations were down. Iverson wrote:

A memory that will stay in my head always is using a 75' aerial bucket truck to 'beat' the ice off a large transmission switch by St. Olaf Lake substation. The wind was blowing so hard that the bucket was swerving as we tried to be patient enough to take a swing at the ice with a hot stick. We finally got the switch open, but for the first time before or since in my working career, you couldn't see an electric light, in any direction, from 75' in the air. I think it was one of the most sobering sights I have ever seen. It was completely dark everywhere. Even the small towns of Ellendale, New Richland, Hope, Freeborn, Hartland were all dark. There was not even a red blinking light on a radio tower or water tower anywhere.

"We know how to take care of a disaster, but this was of a magnitude that we had never faced before," said Jerry Mikel, who at the time was assistant general manager. "Doug Hughes had a battle plan," said Mikel regarding assessment of the damage. "We had retired people that came in and helped us with that." The office staff continued

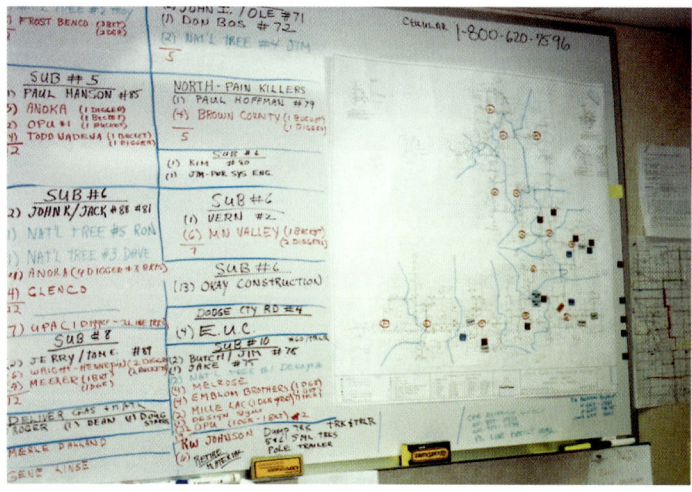

Coordination would be critical in efficiently utilizing the crews and equipment made available to the co-op to restore service. (*SWCE file photo*.)

Working conditions were brutal as high winds magnified the impact of the snow and ice. (*SWCE file photo*.)

The air would be thick with exhaust at the Rose Street office as sixty-seven trucks representing nineteen cooperatives, utilities, or construction crews would prepare for each day during the outages associated with the 1991 Halloween storm. (*SWCE file photo*.)

The Kitchen at the corner of North Cedar and Rose Street was where the crews typically met to start their day. Mary Crippner and her crew would open early to serve breakfast to the linemen. The Kitchen also prepared noon lunches of hot soup and beverages that were delivered by the board of directors, their wives, and co-op management staff to the repair crews so they could be fed without leaving a job site. (*SWCE file photo*.)

to man the phones through the night aided by linemen's wives and friends.

Saturday morning began with a 5 a.m. breakfast at The Kitchen for the eighty-plus linemen who had arrived from various parts of the state. They would work in incredible conditions through the day with winds gusting up to 64 mph. "You'd get out of the truck and the wind was strong, it'd

just take you right down," said retired Crew Chief Vern Schlobohm. "It was so slippery, you couldn't stand up." The heaviest hit areas included a path starting around ten miles west of Ellendale, crossing north of Owatonna, then northeast. At the height of the battle, 127 men and 67 line trucks representing 19 cooperatives, utilities, or construction crews were on hand to help. "Without them it would have been almost impossible to battle," said Mikel. "It just shows the cooperative family at its best." Larson knew the process would be helped if everything was brought to the crews, "I called the board and said, 'You're going to work.'" Meals prepared by The Kitchen were delivered by the board of directors and their families. "Everybody worked – everybody stayed put," said Larson. The office staff provided coordination, and poles and hardware were delivered on site.

"We carried socks. We carried mittens and gloves and I don't know what other clothes we had along, but guys were all wet. They would change in the truck or car, put on dry and they went back to work," recalled now retired board director Don Resler. On Monday, seven of fourteen substations went back online. By Tuesday, the long hours

Weather conditions combined with the duration of repairs challenged each man in the field. (*SWCE file photo.*)

and the elements were taking their toll. Linemen's faces were raw from the cold and wind, lips were cracked and fingers split open from working in the elements. Co-op employees continued to put in long hours and most didn't leave the office until 10 p.m. or later. Regular business had to be handled throughout the crisis. By late Wednesday, the majority of Steele-Waseca members had electricity. Thursday was the final day for crews that came to assist. Some would go assist Freeborn-Mower Cooperative Electric with their battle to restore power from the storm. "I still can't believe they got all those lines up in a week – it was just unbelievable," said Schlobohm. On Saturday, problems occurred for Steele-Waseca when ice was falling off the lines causing outages.

On the heels of the Halloween storm in 1991, icy rain applied a thick glaze on the power lines on Friday, November 29. Crews began arriving at 4 p.m. and worked through the night trying to

Gege Abraham was among the office employees who put in long days not only to assist with the outage, but to handle the regular duties of daily business. (*SWCE file photo.*)

keep up with the many outages. Steele-Waseca served sixty townships throughout their service and nearly all of them had outages. Crews that had assisted during the Halloween storm returned. The crew totaled fifty-four people, plus all the office employees and volunteers. During the Halloween storm, four hundred distribution poles and twenty-five large transmission poles had to be replaced. This storm had around twenty poles and twenty crossarms that need to be replaced, but hundreds of wire breaks. By Sunday, many had their power restored. Crews stayed through Monday to clean up the enormous amount of debris such as fallen trees and limbs. Blizzard conditions were present on Tuesday, but to the relief of the co-op very few outages were reported.

District 6 Director Don Starks retired from the board at the annual meeting in 1992. Gary Wilson was elected by the membership in attendance to replace him. District 2 Director George Byron and District 4 Director Lyle Wayne were re-elected.

The annual meeting in 1993 attracted nine hundred members to the Four Seasons Centre in Owatonna. Robert Malecha retired as director with Kenneth Mracek elected by the members to replace him. Jake Gillen was elected over Sylvester Emge and Donald Kolb was re-elected for another three-year term. At the reorganizational meeting Don Resler was elected board president.

The co-op's finance division led by Dave Lundberg had been put in charge of preparing damage estimates from the 1991 Halloween storm for the Federal Emergency Management Agency (FEMA), a process that took two years. FEMA would eventually deliver financial assistance for the cooperative for repairs to the system. Mikel recalled a meeting in the boardroom with State Senator Dave Durenburger and officials with FEMA who were arguing over how much would be needed for repairs to Steele-Waseca's system. According to Mikel, Durenburger leaned back in his chair and said, "I've known these REA people for a lot of years and if they say it's true, you can believe them." Mikel said the meeting was over and FEMA fulfilled the co-op's requests, "It was well worth our effort. We learned about FEMA and we made very sure that they knew about us." Larson wrote in the January 1994 *Sparks*, "We have finally finished up the main damage from the ice storms of 1991. We will receive $2,059,000 from FEMA to assist us, but we had to invest an additional $1 million plus over a two year period to restore our system to a high reliability standard."

Steele-Waseca's experience with the 1991 Halloween storm arguably was the push that led the board of directors to pursue the need for a new facility. "The storm actually allowed us to look to build," said retired board director Don Resler. "We knew we had growth. With the grant money from FEMA, it put us in a good position to look to build." Adding, "We knew we had to do something because the other building was not big enough anymore. And we didn't have any storage."

For Resler, it was also about what he witnessed during the 1991 Halloween storm, "I had made a promise to myself that we're going to build a building

> # Steele-Waseca's experience with the 1991 Halloween storm arguably was the push that led the board of directors to pursue the need for a new facility.

for the guys to work in. After '91, when I seen what they did, what they had to work with under all those conditions that were out there, and nobody really bitched about it. I couldn't believe that there wasn't some because they were wet and cold."

The decision for the board was not easy as there were still concerns about the cost to build new versus remodeling the old. The cooperative would find an agreeable land purchase at the corner of 24th Avenue Southwest and West Bridge Street. Tim Peterson of Architectural Design Group in Menomonie, Wisconsin, was selected as the architect for the project. Excavation work started September 16, 1993. The general contractor was Rocon, Inc., of Owatonna; plumbing was through McCarthy Plumbing & Heating, Inc., of Owatonna; the sprinkler system was installed by Viking Sprinkler of St. Paul; the HVAC system was installed by KSW Roofing & Heating, Inc., of Owatonna; the electrical work was completed by M&M Electrical, Inc., of New Richland; the landscaper was Helen's Turf & Tree of Medford; and painting and wall covering work was completed by Apex Painting Company.

Meanwhile, Steele-Waseca continued to upgrade their substations as needed. On October 18, 1993, Steele-Waseca crew members John Kucera, Jerry Lewison, Jim Wolters, Don Bos, Kevin Sedivy, Jake Jacobson, Roger Rehman, and Wehner Crane of Austin unloaded a 5,000-kilovolt-amp, 38,000-pound transformer at Sub 6–Bixby. The total electrical load south and east of Owatonna had grown to the point the Bixby substation required upgrading. The transformers and regulators from the Bixby sub would eventually be moved to the Riverpoint substation, twelve miles south of Owatonna on County Road 45. The Riverpoint transformers and regulators would be installed in the new French Lake substation. In addition, plans for Sub 16 in Faribault's Airtech Park started in September 1993. The transmission line voltages would be higher than the typical 69 kilovolts and would be constructed to carry 115

A groundbreaking ceremony for the present office was conducted August 27, 1993. (*SWCE file photo.*)

Crew Chief Jerry Lewison makes final the connections to lift a 38,000-pound transformer. (*SWCE* Sparks *newsletter, January 1994.*)

TOP: KSW Roofing & Heating installing PVC heat transfer pipe in the ground on November 3, 1993. (*Photo by Doug Hughes.*)

BOTTOM: The Wirsbo heating system was installed in the garage and warehouse area during March 1994. The concrete was then poured over the plastic tubing for radiant floor heating that produces an even temperature from the floor to the ceiling. (*Photo by Doug Hughes.*)

kilovolts to serve industries like IFP and K-Bar. The substation would be energized in December 1998.

As of November 1, 1993, most of the excavating work at the new office site had been completed. Sewer, water, and telephone lines were installed. The tiling of the property was completed with footings to be laid early in November. The delivery date for the steel to be used in the roof and office portions was delayed. KSW Roofing & Heating laid 33,000 feet of PVC transfer pipe in the ground, which for KSW at the time was the largest ground

water system they had ever installed. It would utilize thirteen heat pumps to heat and cool the Steele-Waseca office and facilities. The ground water heat pumps allowed the co-op to heat and cool the facility at a fraction of the cost of a regular heating and cooling system.

In February 1994, the crews set up heaters in the buildings to take the frost out of the ground so the ground water loop system could be installed and concrete poured. During the first week of June 1994, the front sidewalks and driveways were

Prisoners from the state prison in Faribault constructed the cabinetry in the new office and installed the eighteen-foot boardroom table donated by Director Harold Amley and his wife, Jean. (*Photo by Doug Hughes.*)

poured, the front door was installed, the installation of cabinets began, and the painters started work in the office. The garage and warehouse portion of the new facility was turned over to the co-op in mid-June. Retired Line Foreman Jerry Lewison said the new facility made "a world of difference" to the efficiency for the line crews. With space needs at the Rose Street facility, hardware for the crews was at their pole yard on East School Street. "We'd spend a lot of time just back and forth," said Lewison, while now in fifteen minutes the crew could be prepared for the day. "I think it saved the company a lot of money by moving out here."

Over nine hundred members were in attendance for the annual meeting on June 7, 1994. With Director Joe Fox retiring, David J. Clausen of Freedom Township in Waseca County was elected in District 1. District 3 Director Harold Amley of

Pancakes were served up at the open house for the new SWCE office. (*Photo by Doug Hughes.*)

Otisco Township in LeSueur County and District 5 Director Donald Resler of Aurora Township in Steele County were re-elected for three-year terms by the members in attendance at the annual meeting.

Steele-Waseca's new office was constructed for $2.5 million. The co-op started conducting

business at their new office on July 20, 1994. A formal open house was held on September 20, 1994, and was attended by over 1,200 members and guests. As for the Rose Street office, it was sold to the Owatonna School District #761 on January 2, 1997.

The Rural Electrification Administration would have its name changed in 1994 to Rural Utilities South Dakota. The ten-million-gallon ethanol plant would be constructed west of Claremont at a cost of $16 million with Steele-Waseca providing electrical service.

After forty-five years of service with Steele-Waseca, General Manager Don Larson at the annual meeting on June 6, 1995, announced his retirement would be January 5, 1996. Members

A 1990s view of the Medford Outlet Center as it was among the co-op's commercial loads added during the decade along the Interstate 35/Medford corridor. (*Photo by Doug Hughes, CFII-MEII.*)

Service (RUS) as services were expanded to include water and sewer. The RUS became one of three units of a new rural development section of the U.S. Department of Agriculture.

On April 17, 1995, a groundbreaking ceremony was conducted in Claremont for the Al-Corn Clean Fuel ethanol plant. The planning process began in 1993 when local farmers, a banker, and Steele-Waseca staff toured an ethanol plant in in attendance approved 319 to 27 a bylaw change for redistricting to provide balance in each of the nine districts as recommended by RUS. Directors George Byron, Lyle Wayne, and Gary Wilson were all re-elected for three-year terms. In September 1995, Director David Clausen resigned in which the board of directors appointed Sylvester Emge to complete the term of the new District 1 which would be up for election at the annual meeting in 1996.

National, state, and local government officials along with local business representatives and residents were on hand for the groundbreaking ceremony for the Al-Corn Clean Fuel ethanol plant. (*SWCE* Sparks *newsletter, July 1995*.)

A view of a completed Al-Corn Clean Fuel plant. (*Photo by Doug Hughes, CFII-MEII*.)

Donald Larson. (*SWCE file photo*.)

Gerald Mikel. (*Photo courtesy of Oldenburg Photography.*)

Co-op employees shared with Don upon his retirement, "You have watched many of us 'grow up' here and have been a fellow employee, and dedicated boss. While you have always demanded excellence from us on the job, you have also understood what is really important in life and that is our families…We wish you and Maxine many years of happiness with your family and friends, and lots of pars on the golf course. We will always cherish your friendship."

Assistant General Manager Jerry Mikel would become the co-op's fourth general manager on January 6, 1996, after thirty-one years with Steele-Waseca. In March of that year, he would implement a process improvement program for the cooperative, which essentially afforded everyone to get better at their job every day. "When we started this, not

everyone wanted to play," said Mikel. "If a lineman had an idea that involved the accounting division, that was fine." Mikel explained a team of employees would be developed to test the proposed plan and then implemented if testing was successful. "Our efficiency went up, our margins went up, cash in the bank went up."

Straight-line winds around 2 a.m. on May 19, 1996, devastated the transmission lines serving Steele-Waseca. General Manager Jerry Mikel wrote, "The comparison of damage on our transmission lines was four-five times worse than we experienced in our 1991 ice storm." The extreme southwest and extreme northeast parts sustained the most violent devastation from the storm. "I personally visited the damaged areas and talked with many of our members as they tried to get their lives back to

Line damage sustained from straight-line winds in the early morning hours of May 19, 1996. (*SWCE file photo*.)

some level of order," wrote Mikel. "Most were just thankful that they were safe, uninjured and that we were working on restoring service." Seven cooperatives and other utilities assisted with manpower, material, and equipment to minimize the outage to forty-four hours. The storm caused over $200,000 in damages for the co-op of which they were able to apply for federal assistance through a disaster declaration.

Breakfast was served to the membership at the June 1996 annual meeting. Members elected Raymond Duchene of Wells Township in Rice County to serve in the newly formed District 1. Incumbent Directors Jake Gillen, Donald Kolb, and Kenneth Mracek were each re-elected for three-year terms.

Steele-Waseca would advance their after-hours dispatch on July 7, 1997, by contracting with Dakota Electric Association and their PORCHE (Primary Outage Response Call Handling Equipment) system. The system continues to be utilized today and allows up to twelve calls to be answered either by electronic voice or a live dispatcher. The previous system for Steele-Waseca involved cooperation with Owatonna Public Utilities, which only allowed one call to be handled at a time.

Over 1,500 attended EnergyFest '98 held on February 21 which featured a craft show, information and demonstration booths, children's corner, and more as a fundraiser for the SW-VPs Scholarship Fund. (*Photo by Doug Hughes*.)

In July 1997, Steele-Waseca hosted an informational meeting at the co-op with surrounding community leaders to explore the potential of the development along Interstate 35W. The recurring subject arose regarded housing needs. Steele-Waseca partnered with the communities of Medford, Blooming Prairie, and Ellendale to form a housing committee. Meanwhile, the Faribault Industrial Park continued to grow with Faribault Foods, Met-Con, McDonough Truck Line, Inc., and others.

The process for billing would change with the September 1997 billing. The printing of the bills would be outsourced and would include the insertion of the *Sparks* newsletter. Members using the inserted envelopes would have their payment sent to a post office box in St. Paul for processing. Payment information and meter readings would be electronically transferred each morning with a courier bringing the actual paperwork in the afternoon. Even though the contracted companies have changed, the process continues to be utilized to this day by Steele-Waseca. In an effort to save money, the co-op stopped mailing late notices regarding payments, but would simply add the delinquent balance to the new bill starting in January 1999. In addition, auto pay and pre-pay programs were promoted in the late 1990s and remain available today.

Steele-Waseca in 1998 would also join the alliance of Touchstone Energy. The alliance, which in 2010 was 550 cooperatives, was formed to enable individual co-ops to share ideas and advanced technologies with other co-ops using a national brand network. Touchstone Energy's values are the same ones cooperative members have come to rely on since the beginning of cooperatives—accountability, integrity, innovation, and community involvement.

Steele-Waseca's membership to Cooperative Power Association (CPA) would be altered on January 1, 1999, as CPA would form an alliance with United Power Association (UPA) to form Great River Energy (GRE). Steele-Waseca would be among twenty-eight distribution cooperatives serviced by the newly formed generation and transmission cooperative. Originally based in Elk River, GRE dedicated their new office in Maple Grove in April 2008.

After decades of members reading their meter, the Steele-Waseca Board of Directors approved the purchase and installation of an automated meter reading system. Turtle® technology developed by Paul Hunt of Hunt Technologies of Pequot Lakes, Minnesota, would allow Steele-Waseca to have installations completed for automated readings that would be sent electronically over the co-op's existing power lines to the co-op office. "Turtle metering puts Steele-Waseca and all co-ops on the cutting edge of technology in the electric utility industry," wrote General Manager Jerry Mikel in the October 1999 *Sparks.* For the members, it would mean convenience of not to having to take the time to read their meter monthly. Mikel wrote, "On our end – the business end – Turtle meters eliminate a step in the billing process. Electronic data replaces paper readings, allows us to manage billing information with even greater accuracy and efficiency, and makes better use of our equipment and human resources." Installations started in 1998 and would continue into 2001.

Technological advances would continue with Steele-Waseca's introduction of their Web site in November 1998. Additional services for members regarding classified advertisements and their account balance were introduced in August 1999.

Steele-Waseca once again started sending delegates to the Washington, D.C. Youth Tour in 1999. The program would be open to sophomores or juniors who were dependents of a Steele-Waseca member. The event continues today and is organized by the Minnesota Rural Electric Association and hosted by the National Rural Electric Cooperative Association. ■

Your Touchstone Energy® Cooperative
The power of human connections®

(Courtesy Touchstone Energy.)

11

2000 to Present

After coming through the speculated challenges of Y2K and entering the twenty-first century, technology was not only delegated to internal office operations. Substations were being monitored by computer equipment and line crews were being equipped with equipment, cell phone technology, and other tools from hydraulics to lights that allowed safer, more productive work in less time, and in the end, at less cost.

The number of scholarship recipients was able to increase through the SW-VPs raffle and other special events hosted by the cooperative. From 1999 to 2001, five $500 scholarships were awarded yearly to dependents of Steele-Waseca members. The applications were judged on academic achievement, school and community activities, and an essay.

After closing the 1990s by serving breakfast at the annual meeting, the June 6, 2000, annual meeting was a late afternoon affair, which drew over 1,400 members and guests to the Four Seasons Centre. Incumbent Directors Raymond Duchene, Harold Amley, and Donald Resler were re-elected for three-year terms. The highlight of the event was guest speaker, Bill LaMacchia Jr., president and CEO of Sun Country Airlines, who talked about the growth of the airline in a deregulated environment. The prize drawings included eight, $250 Sun Country Airlines tickets.

Steele-Waseca's Marathon water heater program would debut in June 2000. By joining the co-op's interruptible water heating program, the member would be eligible to receive a free Marathon water heater.

Gordie Schroeder retired after thirty-four years with Steele-Waseca on February 26, 2002. He started his career as a truck driver-groundman on February 26, 1968, and retired as the operations division manager. "The transition from lineman to working in the office was one of my greatest challenges. As load management coordinator, I was responsible for developing SWCE's off-peak program, which was a huge change from lineman work. I was very fortunate to have Doug Hughes to work with on that program."

Line crews battled the impacts of an ice storm March 14–16, 2002. The ice forced lines to break causing outages and then when the weather warmed, ice falling from the lines caused the lines to collide, which resulted in more broken wires and outages.

Steele-Waseca's sixty-sixth annual meeting on June 4, 2002, would be the first at their headquarters on West Bridge Street in Owatonna with eight hundred members and guests in attendance. Incumbent Directors Donald Kolb and Kenneth Mracek were re-elected. John Beal was elected over incumbent Jake Gillen in District 7.

In 2002, the cooperative financed fifteen, $350 scholarships, mostly through unclaimed capital credit equity. The scholarship amount grew to $500 in 2004 and remains at that level today. The only change that has occurred since that time is the schools administer the selection of their individual recipient. The co-op only requires the graduating high school student is a dependent of a Steele-Waseca member and the recipient is attending a two- or four-year postsecondary institution. In total, $94,250 in scholarships have been awarded since 1954.

Gordie Schroeder. (*SWCE file photo*.)

OPPOSITE PAGE: Steele-Waseca Master Electrician Mark McDonald helps promote the Marathon water heater program during the 2001 annual meeting. (*SWCE file photo*.)

Thanks for lending a GreenTouch!

The statewide GreenTouch effort of more than 300 Touchstone Energy Cooperative volunteers helped spruce up Minnesota State Parks on May 6, 2000. Locally, about 35 people, including Steele-Waseca members and friends, active and retired employees and their families, and Cub Scout Pack #350 from Medford all helped at Rice Lake State Park. 16790

We painted gates, scraped and painted picnic tables, trimmed trees, cleared rocks and cattails, installed a new gate, and cleaned trails and park grounds. (see photo)

Roger Heimgartner, Rice Lake State Park Ranger says, "Thanks many times over! Your help has more value than most people realize. Due to budget cuts, we no longer have the staff to do all these projects ourselves."

We had more projects than time, so there'll be plenty to do on the next GreenTouch workday. Thanks, again!

(SWCE *Sparks* newsletter, June 2000.)

Steele-Waseca line crews work to repair the lines and get service restored. (*SWCE file photo*.)

INSET: A measurement of the ice that had built up on the lines as a result of the March 2002 ice storm. (*SWCE file photo*.)

Steele-Waseca conducted their first annual meeting at their new headquarters in 2002. The annual meeting has since been held at the same venue. (*Photo by Doug Hughes*.)

The cooperative was continuing to experience growth in 2002 with housing developments in Lonsdale. Line crews were installing underground facilities in the developments of Harvest Pond, Maple Shores, Rolling Ridge, and Willow Creek Heights. Steele-Waseca's wholesale energy provider, Great River Energy (GRE), in 2003 passed on the costs of two peaking plants to its twenty-eight member cooperatives. The peaking plants were constructed at a cost of about $500 million to avoid the volatile open market for power purchases needed during peak usage times. In addition, residual effects of the September 11, 2001, terrorist attacks were still being felt with increasing costs for liability insurance for companies like GRE.

To promote energy efficiency, ENERGY STAR rebates were introduced in 2003 for central air conditioners, air and ground source heat pumps, refrigerators, dishwashers, and clothes washers. The ENERGY STAR rebate program continues today for Steele-Waseca members.

Nearly one thousand members and guests were in attendance for the annual meeting on June 3, 2003. Director Harold Amley retired and Duane Edwardson was elected by the members to serve District 3. Incumbent Directors Raymond Duchene and Donald Resler were re-elected for three-year terms. At the reorganizational meeting, Resler stepped down as president and Donald Kolb was elected board president; John Beal was elected vice president.

On August 26, 2003, the board of directors approved a resolution to offer members the Wellspring wind energy program. The program would allow members to purchase blocks of 100 kilowatt-hours of wind energy not exceeding their own usage and in addition to their normal electric rate. The price in 2003 was $1.45 per 100-kilowatt-hour block. In 2010, the rate was $0.40 per 100-kilowatt-hour block.

The Wellspring Wind Energy program allows Steele-Waseca members to contribute toward increased renewable energy purchases for the cooperative.

Products with the ENERGY STAR label have met government specifications regarding energy efficiency. (*Logo courtesy of ENERGY STAR.*)

Sub #17 was constructed on land Steele-Waseca purchased from Al-Corn Clean Fuel. (*SWCE* Sparks *newsletter, December 2003.*)

ACRE participation is voluntary, but provides support of federal political candidates that protect the interests of rural electric cooperatives and their members.

Dennis Ringhofer and Geraldine Lienke were elected to the board of directors at Steele-Waseca's sixty-eighth annual meeting. (*SWCE file photo*.)

Steele-Waseca Attorney John McLoone IV retired at the end of 2004. He was legal counsel to the co-op for over thirty-two years. His father, John McLoone III, also had previously served as legal counsel to Steele-Waseca. (*SWCE file photo*.)

The co-op's latest sub, Al-Corn Substation #17, was energized October 29, 2003. The sub is located on four acres directly south of Al-Corn Clean Fuel ethanol plant. The sub increased service and reliability and provides for future industrial, commercial, and residential demand growth in the Claremont area. The sub was designed so the structures are lower, making maintenance easier to perform and its appearance more visually pleasing. The transmission voltage supplying the new sub-station is 161 kilovolts, which is more than any other sub on Steele-Waseca's system. Assistance with the construction came from United Services Group, Utili-Trax, Inc., and Great River Energy. Among those providing additional load for the co-op during the 2000s would be Medford Public School, Aldi

Warehouse, Sage Electrochromics of Faribault, and Ritchie Bros. Auctioneers of Medford.

Steele-Waseca's general managers and board of directors have maintained contact through the years with their elected representatives regarding legislation and policies impacting the cooperative. In 2004, Steele-Waseca members were informed of ACRE (Action Committee for Rural Electrification). ACRE was established in 1966 by the National Rural Electric Cooperative Association and organized to support only the political candidates who support and protect the interests of rural electric members and their cooperatives. Membership is voluntary and open to all members desiring to join.

More than 830 members and guests were in attendance for the annual meeting on June 8, 2004.

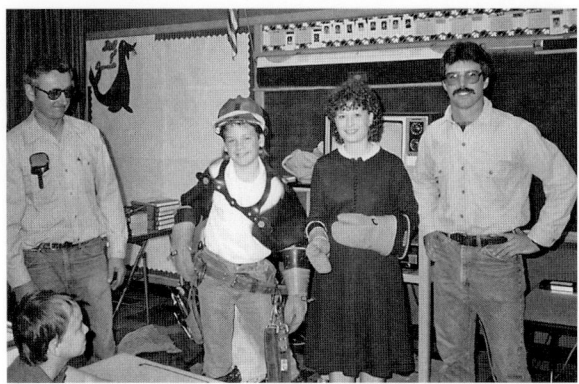

John Kucera presented countless electrical safety seminars to youth during his career at Steele-Waseca. Kucera (left) and Paul Becker conduct a session to fourth graders in New Richland in April 1988 as a student and teacher wore the linemen's gear. (*SWCE file photo*.)

Some long-time members still remember the red trucks operated by the cooperative to service the poles and lines. Technology prompted the cooperative to invest in remote-controlled digger trucks as being utilized by one of the co-op's current linemen, Justin Bergeson (pictured right). (*SWCE file photo*.)

Linemen Jack Schwab (left) and Nordean Hartle are pictured near the co-op's bucket truck among the debris in the Franklington, Louisiana area devastated by Hurricane Katrina. (*SWCE file photo*.)

Co-op members elected their first woman to serve on the board of directors as Geraldine Lienke was elected in District 2. She replaced George Byron who retired from the board. In District 4, Dennis Ringhofer was elected as Lyle Wayne also retired from the board of directors. Incumbent Gary Wilson was re-elected in District 6. Wilson earlier in the year was elected to represent Steele-Waseca on the Great River Energy Board of Directors.

After nearly thirty-eight years, Line Foreman John Kucera retired on July 31, 2004. He started as a truck driver-groundman on December 5, 1966, and worked his way up to apprentice line technician, line technician, crew chief, and foreman until serving as line foreman until his retirement. His memories include working nearly non-stop through the 1991 ice storms, moving to the West Bridge Street location, and working for three different general managers during his career.

Steele-Waseca raised rates in January 2005 due to rising wholesale power prices and higher costs for maintenance, equipment, transportation, fuel, labor, and insurance along with a reduction in investment income for the cooperative. The rate increase averaged about $7.75 per month per member.

Steele-Waseca embraced the latest technology in 2005 with the purchase of their first remote controlled digger truck, which allows linemen to operate the digger while standing on the ground rather than sitting on a chair on top of the truck. The remote technology makes excavating easier and faster, and keeps linemen safer because it eliminates the chance of a blind spot during operation. "We want them to have the best and latest technology," said Director John Beal. "If it makes your job easier and makes it safer…We are also open to new technology as it comes along."

One of the seven cooperative principles is cooperation among cooperatives. Linemen Jack Schwab and Nordean Hartle represented Steele-Waseca as

Gerald Mikel. (*Photo courtesy of Oldenburg Photography.*)

they and twenty-six other linemen representing ten Minnesota electric co-ops traveled to Franklington, Louisiana, on September 23, 2005, to help restore power to the homes, farms, and businesses of Washington-St. Tammany Electric Cooperative devastated by Hurricane Katrina. The monster storm destroyed an estimated 3,500 miles of power lines and left nearly 45,000 of the co-op's members without power. Workdays in the hot weather were fourteen to sixteen hours long. By the end of October 3, Washington-St. Tammany had restored power to 100 percent of their members ready to accept power. Hundreds of the co-op's members had sustained too much damage to have power restored until they had time to make necessary repairs.

Approximately 910 members and guests were in attendance for the co-op's seventieth annual meeting. With the retirement of Director Donald Resler, Kenneth Prestegard was elected in District 5. Incumbents Duane Edwardson and Raymond Duchene were re-elected for three-year terms.

Straight-line winds left approximately 1,500 Steele-Waseca members without power on July 31, 2008. Approximately 90 percent of all the outages involved downed trees that took down power lines. Initial outages were created when the French Lake substation lost power due to a transmission pole that went down southwest of the substation. In addition, Steele-Waseca line crews replaced three power poles damaged by wind. Approximately three hundred members had their power restored by 5 p.m. the following day. Special thanks went out to Carr's Tree Service and the assistance received from the Goodhue and Freeborn-Mower cooperatives.

General Manager Jerry Mikel announced his intent to retire before the membership at the 2008 annual meeting. His final day would be January 5, 2009, with over forty-four years of service with Steele-Waseca. "His vision, level of dedication, and his relationship with the members and the entire board of directors will greatly be missed," wrote Board President Donald Kolb. "Jerry has been a strong leader who has continually developed a positive relationship

Syd Briggs joined Steele-Waseca on January 6, 2009. (*Photo courtesy of Oldenburg Photography.*)

with the cooperative family. His knowledge and expertise has given this co-op a strong position in today's world and we thank him for those contributions."

Steele-Waseca's current General Manager Syd Briggs came from Southwest Arkansas Electric Cooperative in Texarkana, Arkansas, where he served as their vice president of accounting, finance, and member services. Having grown up in Del Rio, Texas, Briggs began his rural electric career in 1991 with Rio Grande Electric Cooperative where he worked as their director of accounting and finance for eleven years. He and his wife, Tammy, today live in Owatonna. Besides trying to keep members' rates in check despite legislation threatening to increase the cost of electricity, Briggs has participated in renewable energy seminars hosted by Steele-Waseca and started up town hall meetings again for the members to become more informed of the issues impacting their cooperative.

During the 2000s, members would have the opportunity to pay their bill through Steele-Waseca's Web site. Updated in 2010, members may now acquire e-mail notifications regarding their account and access more detailed information and opportunities to participate in various programs through Steele-Waseca.

Storms and tornadic winds on June 17, 2010, caused power outages to 2,516 meter locations largely in the area of Ellendale and Blooming Prairie, including Summit and Berlin townships. Steele-Waseca line crews were assisted by Highline Construction, Inc., of Paynesville on June 18 in replacing approximately sixty poles damaged from the storm. Retired Line Foreman Jerry Lewison provided assistance by reporting damage assessments to the cooperative. Single-phase power was restored to those locations that could handle power by 10:30 p.m., Saturday, June 19. Brief outages took place the following day as three-phase electrical service was restored.

Flooding that started impacting southern Minnesota on September 23, 2010, prompted a shutdown of Sub #2 just north of Owatonna. With the location of the substation adjacent to a flood plain and to avoid any future recurrence, the decision was made to decommission the sub and increase the capability of the nearby substation in Merton Township.

TOP: Storm damage on June 17, 2010, between Blooming Prairie and Ellendale. (*SWCE file photo*.)

BOTTOM: Overhead view of the flooding damage at Sub 2, north of Owatonna. (*Photo by Doug Hughes, CFII-MEII*.)

In closing, Line Foreman John Iverson perhaps put it best when he wrote, "There have been vast improvements in hardware and materials of course, but some very far sighted REA designers in Washington D.C. put together line building that is still basic today – an A-1 structure in 1937 is still an A-1 structure in 2011, all over the REC's across the country. That is quite a tribute to longevity." ■

12

General Managers and Board of Directors

Five general managers have led Steele-Waseca Cooperative Electric in its first seventy-five years. The following is a list of their years of service and a board of directors photo taken during their tenure.

Within the nine county area that Steele-Waseca serves, the following is the list of men and women who have dedicated years of service on the board of directors:

FIRST NAME	LAST NAME	YEARS OF SERVICE	FIRST NAME	LAST NAME	YEARS OF SERVICE
Harold	Amley	1985–2003	Arvid	Sponberg	1936–1937
Jay	Beal	1953–1981	Edward	Springer	1936–1941
John	Beal	2002–present	Donald	Starks	1986–1992
George	Byron	1983–2004	Albert J.	Tuma	1939–1968
Alex	Chambers	1936–1939	E. P.	Underwood	1960–1973
Norbert	Chmelik	1968–1986	Charles B.	Wallace	1938–1953
David	Clausen	1994–1995	Lyle	Wayne	1967–2004
Edward	Doyle	1937–1971	Manford	Wayne	1962–1967
Raymond	Duchene	1996–present	Alois	Wencl	1947–1960
Duane	Edwardson	2003–present	Gary	Wilson	1992–present
Sylvester	Emge	1981–1993, 1995–1996			
Joseph	Fox	1971–1994			
Jake	Gillen	1993–2002			
John A.	Hartle	1953–1968			
A. Chester	Johnson	1961–1966			
Arthur B.	Johnson	1936–1962			
Frank	Johnson	1936			
Allan	Kasper	1936–1938			
Donald	Kolb	1983–present			
Arnold	Larson	1941–1953			
Geraldine	Lienke	2004–present			
A. A.	Lynch	1936			
Robert L.	Malecha	1969–1993			
Kenneth	Mracek	1993–present			
Barney W.	Nicklawske	1936–1947			
Kenneth	Prestegard	2006–present			
Donald	Resler	1973–2006			
Dennis	Ringhofer	2004–present			
Stewart J.	Root	1936–1950			
Milford	Rugroden	1966–1985			
Elmer	Scheffert	1950–1983			
Chris	Shurson	1936–1961			
Ted	Skluzacek	1968–1969			
Donald	Sommers	1938–1983			

The board of directors following the 1945 annual meeting include (seated, left to right): Arthur B. Johnson, Ellendale; Arnold Larson, Claremont; A. J. Tuma, Northfield; and Manager L. P. Zimmerman, Waseca. Standing (L-R): S. J. Root, Matawan; Donald Sommers, Northfield; Chris Shurson, New Richland; Edward Doyle, Waldorf; Attorney G. P. Madden; Barney W. Nicklawske, Owatonna; and Chas. Wallace, Dundas. (*Photo submitted by Ronald Sommers; photographer B. W. Johnson, Owatonna.*)

OPPOSITE PAGE: Louis P. Zimmerman, 1937–1948.

The board of directors following the 1950 annual meeting include (seated, left to right): Edward V. Doyle, president; Arnold L. Larson, secretary-treasurer; Charlie Wallace, vice president; and John McLoone, attorney. Standing (L-R): Arthur B. Johnson, Donald Sommers, Alois Wencl, Chris Shurson, Elmer Scheffert, Albert Tuma, and Howard L. McKee, manager. (*Photo courtesy of Johnson Studio, Owatonna*.)

INSET: Howard L. McKee, 1949–1972.

The board of directors pictured in 1976 include (seated, left to right): Donald Sommers, president; Joseph Fox, vice president; Robert Malecha, secretary-treasurer; and Jay Beal. Standing (L-R): Donald Resler, Milford Rugroden, Elmer Scheffert, General Manager Donald Larson, Lyle Wayne, Norbert Chmelik, and John McLoone IV, attorney. (*SWCE file photo*.)

INSET: Donald B. Larson, 1972–1996.

The board of directors following the 2001 annual meeting include (seated, left to right): Harold Amley, chaplain, District 3; Donald Kolb, vice president, District 8; Donald Resler, president, District 5; Gary Wilson, secretary-treasurer, District 6; and Lyle Wayne, GRE director, District 4. Standing (L-R): John McLoone IV, SWCE attorney; Raymond Duchene, District 1; Jake Gillen, District 7; Kenneth Mracek, District 9; George Byron, District 2; Debbie Eby, administrative assistant; and Gerald Mikel, general manager. (*Photo courtesy of Oldenburg Photography.*)

INSET: Gerald J. Mikel, 1996–2009.

The board of directors pictured in 2010 include (seated, left to right): Duane Edwardson, District 3; Gary Wilson, secretary-treasurer, GRE director, District 6; Donald Kolb, president, District 8; Raymond Duchene, vice president, District 1; and Dennis Ringhofer, assistant secretary/treasurer, District 4. Standing (L-R): Eric Mattison, SWCE attorney; Kenneth Mracek, chaplain, District 9; John Beal, District 7; Kenneth Prestegard, District 5; Geraldine Lienke, District 2; Debbie Eby, executive assistant; and Syd Briggs, general manager. (*Photo courtesy of Oldenburg Photography.*)

INSET: Syd Briggs, 2009–present.

Steele-Waseca's Employees

In seventy-five years, Steele-Waseca has been blessed by the following men and women who committed themselves to serving the membership. The following are lists of the past and present employees, the position(s) they served, and their years of service. The lists were compiled from accessible records and may not have complete information of every employee.

PAST EMPLOYEES:

FIRST NAME	LAST NAME	POSITION	YEARS OF SERVICE
Georgiana	Abraham	Customer Service Representative	1987–2004
Ben	Alrick	Lineman	2004–2008
David	Anderson	Manager of Purchasing and Stores	1974–1989
Dean R.	Andresen	PT Truck Washer	1968, 1969
Genevieve	Andrews	Office Helper	1944
Bernice	Arvig	Bookkeeper/Office Manager	1940–1946
C. C.	Arvig	Stockman	1940
J. E.	Balzer	Farmer/Groundman	1944
Joe	Bartz	Lineman	2002–2007
Paul	Becker	Lineman	1982–1989
Marie	Bedney	General Office Help	1941
Matthew	Bell	Temporary Apprentice Lineman	2006
Derek	Benson	Apprentice Lineman	2004
Leon	Blaha	Line Foreman	1948–1986
Allan G.	Blaker	Groundman	1958, 1959
Fred	Blouin	Janitor	1951
David L.	Bock	Truck Washer	1965–1967
Orville	Bode	Groundman	1948
Donald	Boeke	Groundman	1950
Richard	Bosshard	Groundman	1950
Alice J.	Bowers	Assistant Bookkeeper	1936
D. M.	Boyce	Groundman	1949
Delbert	Brase	Groundman	1947
James	Brase	Temporary Apprentice Lineman	1992
Chris	Bredlow	Groundman	1956
Viona R.	Brink	Assistant Cashier	1967–1969
Ryan	Brockway	Temporary Apprentice Lineman	2010
Allen B.	Brones	Truck Driver/Apprentice Lineman	1963
Fred	Buboltz	Office Helper/Stockman	1942–1943
J. H.	Buck	Groundman	1944
Curtis C.	Bullard	Bookkeeper/Office Manager	1949–1965
John	Burma	Groundman	1950–1965 Summers
Leo	Bushlock	Groundman	1943
Thomas P.	Byrne	Temporary Groundman	1953, 1954
Henry	Cammock	General Foreman	1949–1971
Michael	Cammock	Car Washer	1964
Catherine	Carlson	PT Cooperative Assistant	2004–2005
Lee	Carlson	Programmer/Analyst	1984–1991
Joe F.	Cecha		1942
George	Cervenka	Groundman	1943
Elmer	Chester	Line Helper	1941
Ferris	Chladek	Truck Driver/Groundman	1948–1982
E.	Christianson	Groundman	1944
Joyce	Ciffra	Data Processing	1991–1992
J. E.	Cigrang	Groundman	1943
C. W.	Cofer	Maintenance	1949
Leland	Coulter	Storekeeper/Building and Grounds	1969–1988
Mary Beth	Cox	Receptionist/Operations Clerk	1999–2003
Chad	Dahme	Temporary Apprentice Lineman	1995

Andrew	Dammel	PT Line Personnel	1979
Richard Lee	DeMoss	PT Building Maintenance	1969
Henry	DeRaad	Data Processing Assistant / Member Services	1968–1974
Dale	Detjen	Member Services Director	1966–1987
Russel R.	Dillon	Groundman	1944
Rachel	Dinse	PT Secretary	1984
A.	Dohrmann	Groundman	1944
T. A.	Dornquast	Janitor	1956
Eugene	Douglas	Groundman	1950
Carl	Drache	Truck Driver/Line Foreman	1965–1997
Josena A.	Drews	Cashier	1956–1961
Steven	Dudley	Engineer	2000
Fred	Dumke	Groundman	1943
Charles W.	Duncan	PT Truck Washer	1973, 1975
Erma T.	Dunlop	Bookkeeper	1956–1965
Leonard	Dybevich		1942
Stan	Eaton	Groundman/Line Foreman	1952–1989
Delores	Ebeling	Stockwoman	1943
Brittany	Ellingson	Cooperative Assistant	2006
Edward	Engbard	Storeroom	1946–1950
E. H.	Engle	Easement Man	1940
Dean	Erdman	Groundman/Apprentice Lineman	1947–1987
Gary	Erdman	Car Washer	1961
Thomas	Erickson	Lineman	1989–1993
Keith F.	Fawcett, Jr.	Lineman	1949–1953
H.	Fennert	Farmer/Groundman	1944
N. D.	Ferrington	Groundman	1944
Richard	Fleener	Lineman/Crew Foreman	1940–1975
Charles (Chuck)	Floeter	Apprentice Lineman	1997–1998
Leonard	Flom	Line Helper	1941
Herman	Frahman	Temporary Labor/Janitor	1955–1969
Nicholas	Francis	Temporary Apprentice Lineman	2002
Howard	Frederick	Helper/Lineman	
Rick	Fredin	Apprentice Lineman	1992
Margaret	Frost	Executive Secretary	1942–1980
Orpha	Gage	Typist	
R. C.	Gentry	Stock Clerk	1951
Percy	Giesler	Lineman	1945–1975
Norman	Goertz	Groundman	1950
W. B.	Grait	Groundman	1944
Vernon	Greenwaldt	Lineman	1987–2001
David F.	Grimm	Groundman	1959, 1960, 1961, 1962
Roy	Grunwald		
George	Habeck		1943
Harlan	Habeck	Groundman	1950
E.	Hagerty	Farmer	1944
Ira	Hagerty	Farmer	1944
John	Haigh	Temporary Groundman	1952, 1953, 1954, 1955, 1956
H. C.	Halstenson	Groundman	1944
Clayton	Hanson	Groundman	1944

Edward	Hanson	Lineman	1950–1953, 1956–1974
Karl	Harfmann	Programmer/Operator	1992–1997
Gary J.	Hawkins	Groundman	1962, 1963
Joe	Hawkins	Helper/Lineman/Crew Foreman	1939–1971
Lucille	Hawkins	Stenographer	1940
Pat	Hawkins	Groundman	1942
Daryel	Hendrickson	Groundman	1951–1952
Marie	Heuerman	Office Helper	1944
A.	Hinz	Groundman	1944
Lyle V.	Hoaglund	Truck Driver/Groundman / Apprentice Lineman	1962–1963
Mary	Hodgdon	Bill Machine Operator	1947
Harvey	Hogate	Groundman	1944
William E.	Holden	Temporary Groundman	1955, 1956, 1957, 1958
Frieda M.	Fritze-Holta	Assistant Cashier	1952–1954
Kenneth B.	Holta	Helper/Line Superintendent /Engineer	1940–1955
Virginia	Hughes	PT Summer/Account Clerk /Secretary	1974, 1975, 1976
H.	Hunt	Farmer	1944
LeRoy	Jacobson	Groundman	1946–1947
Barbara	Jalma	Stenographer/Assistant Cashier	1941–1945
H. H.	Jenson	Groundman	1944
Sandy	Jirele	Staff Assistant	1985–1998
A. B.	Johnson	Groundman	1944
Orvin	Johnson	Lineman	1950
Peter Mark	Johnson	PT Groundman	1978
Harvey A.	Johnston		1942
Dale W.	Jones	PT Truck Washer	1970, 1973
Anthony	Jude	Temporary Apprentice Lineman	2001
Cathy	Kaplan	PT Customer Service	2000–2006
Thomas J.	Karaus, Jr.	PT Truck Washer	1969, 1970
Regina	Krause-Kennedy	Stenographer/Cashier	1941–1955
Walter	Kenny	Groundman	1944
Marjorie	Kidd	General Office Help	1944
David N.	Killen	Truck Driver/Groundman	1967, 1968
Rodney G.	Kinny	Truck Driver/Apprentice Lineman	1963–1968
Roger W.	Kittleson		1966
Eugene F.	Klessig	Truck Washer	1964–1965
E.	Knutson	Farmer	1944
W. M.	Knutson	Groundman	1944
Torrey	Kramer	Lineman	1998–2003
Herbert	Krause	Groundman	1945
Mark B.	Kristo	PT Truck Washer	1969, 1970
John	Kucera	Lineman/Line Foreman	1966–2004
Arnold L.	Larson	Bookkeeper	1936
D.	Larson	Farmer	1944
Donald B.	Larson	Groundman/Meterman/General Manager	1950, 1951–1996
Emma	Larson	General Office Help	1940
Stanton	Larson	Accountant/Office Manager	1965–1991
Katie	Laughlin	Temporary Cooperative Assistant	2009
Terry L.	Lee	Key Punch Operator	1971
Dwight	Lennon	Meterman/Superintendent of Member Services	1949–1951

Gerald	Lewison	Truck Driver/Line Foreman	1968–2007
John	Lonergan	Groundman	1941
D.	Long	Janitor	1944
Albert	Longrehr	Groundman	1943
Bret	Loudy	Temporary Office Assistant	2002
Nicholas A.	Louris	PT Summer Help/Draftsman	1973, 1974
L.	Lufte	Farmer	1944
Barbara	Lutz	Cashier	1969–1974
Duane	Lyke	Lineman	2002
Thomas	Lynch	Lineman	1989–1998
Embart	MacKean	Groundman	1943
Dale E.	Magee	PT Building Maintenance	1968
Tiffany	Malecha	Temporary Cooperative Assistant	2010
Clinton L.	Matson	PT Summer Help Painter	1970, 1971
Justin	Matson	Apprentice Lineman	1995–1999
Marlene	Mayhew	Computer Operator	1992–1995
Barret	McClaskie	Temporary Apprentice Lineman	2010
Vern	McGregor	Office Manager	1946–1951
Veronica	McGuiness	Typist	1948–1954
Howard	McKee	Groundman/General Manager	1949–1972
Howard L.	McKee, Jr.	Meter Tester	1955
John	McKelvey	PT Building Maintenance	1968, 1969
William E.	McKinstry	PT Truck Washer	1968
Mary	McManee		
Peter	McNamee	Janitor	1951–1955
Michelle	Meixner	PT	1992
Jodi	Mens	PT Engineering Secretary	1988–1990
Gerald	Mikel	Data Processing Manager/ General Manager	1964–2008
Garret P.	Miller	Truck Washer	1967
Milo M.	Miner	Mechanic	1959–1969
Alice J.	Mittlestadt		1949
Stella	Molde	Stock Clerk	1943
William H.	Mork	Apprentice Lineman/Lineman	1946–1958
Frank	Mueller	Groundman	1943
Arthur	Mussman	Groundman	1943
Allen (Butch)	Nelson	Relief Crew Chief	1974–2000
Betty Lou	Nelson	Account Clerk/Executive Secretary	1979–1982
Gerald	Nelson	Meter Department/Groundman/Engineer	1951, 1952, 1954–1959, 1959–1978
Beverly	Neuman	Billing Clerk	1951–1953
B. W.	Nicklawske	Groundman	1943
Eugene	Nicklawske	Maintenance/Director of Operations	1941
Margaret	Nogaj	Assistant Cashier	1946
Blanche	Nye	Secretary/Assistant Cashier	1957–1985
William	Oberstein	Systems Analyst	1975–1991
Betty A.	Oeltjenbruns	Clerical	1955
Beverly A.	Olson	Billing Clerk	1954
E. J.	Panzer	Groundman	1944
Richard	Patrin	Groundman	1977
Ferne	Pavek	Clerical	1949
Kathy	Hake-Peterson	Cashier/Member Services Manager	1974–1996

Selmer	Peterson	Groundman	1943
Phyllis	Pierce	Clerical	1949
G. E.	Pooch	Groundman	1944
Silvine	Pribyl	Substation Guard	1941
L.	Probanz	General Office	1944
John P.	Pumper		1942
Ronald	Ramsey	Shop Supervisor	1969–1991
L.	Reichstetter	Groundman	1944
Betty	Richardson	Assistant Cashier	1945–1946
W. S.	Ripley	First Lineman	1936
Theodore J.	Ritter	Engineer	1954–1967
Russell P.	Roe		1941
Thomas	Rudolf	PT Line Personnel	1979
Gerald R.	Salsbery	Lineman	
Arthur	Schlinger	Groundman/Apprentice Lineman	1943
Vern	Schlobohm	Groundman/Crew Chief	1952–1989
Evelyn	Schmanskl	Stenographer	1942
John	Schmidt	Maintenance Man	1949–1966
Gordon	Schroeder	Truck Driver/Operations Division Manager	1968–2002
Kari	Schroht	Cashier/Secretary	1977–1980
Francis	Schultz	Groundman	1943
Norbert	Schultz	Groundman	1943
Philip	Schultz	Groundman	1943
Floyd	Schuster	Maintenance/Lineman	1943–1976
Kevin	Sedivy	PT Apprentice Lineman /Groundman	1992–1995
S. M.	Seljeseth	Groundman	1944
Herbert	Semmann	Meter Reader	
Walter	Semmann	Lineman	
Veronica	Senskivek	Stenographer	1941
Courtney	Severtson	Temporary Cooperative Assistant	2007
Hannah	Severtson	Temporary Cooperative Assistant	2005–2008
Gerald H.	Sevlie	Groundman	1965
Jeralyn	Sexter	Cashier	1982–1985
Dan	Shea		1942
John W.	Sherman, Jr.	Groundman	1958
Vickie	Skala	Clerk Typist/Executive Assistant	1975–1996
J. A.	Skalicky	Groundman	1944
John P.	Sklusacek		1942
Sandra	Sola	Microfilm Operator/Assistant Cashier	1983–1985
Myron	Sommers	Groundman	1944
Kurt A.	Sortland	PT Summer Help	1973
Gerald	Springer	Groundman	1951, 1952
Fred	Spitzack	Janitor	1949
Thomas	Stanton	Controlled Systems Consultant	1969–1991
Nichols	Stensel	Groundman	1943
C.	Stenson	Groundman	1944
John	Sullivan	Temporary Apprentice Lineman	2007
Brian	Sundquist	Temporary Apprentice Lineman	2001
Carole A.	Swen	Clerical	1955–1957
Mary Lee	Thamert	Assistant Cashier	1954–1955
Zachariah	Theis	Temporary Apprentice Lineman	2004
Cynetta	(Papke) Thiewes	Stenographic/Cashier	1936

Norma	Thompson	General Office Help	1941
Kathleen	Thurnau	Assistant Cashier	1946
L.	Tietz	Groundman	1944
L. H.	Trapp	Groundman	1944
Merrill	Tucker		1949
Darlene	Mollenhauer-Ulrich	Billing Clerk	1954–1956
Terry	Underdahl	Lineman	1992–2000
G.	Vaith	Groundman	1944
Anton	Vavra		1942
Nancee J.	Vavrichek	Clerical	1957
A.	Verplank	Farmer	1944
A. Del	Warden	Groundman	1958
R. A.	Weber		1944
Rownell H.	Weber	Groundman	1950, 1952–1958
Fulton J.	Weckman	Groundman	1960, 1961
Cristine	Weiss	Engineering Secretary	1984
Jim	Whiteis	Janitor	1949–1951
Paul	Wilder	Electrician	1999
Mary M.	Willing	Clerical	1960
Laura	Willis	Data Entry	1995–1997
Jennifer	Wilson	Temporary Cooperative Assistant	2006, 2007, 2009, 2010
Lee P.	Wiuff	Painter	1960
Ronald D.	Wobbrock	Truck Driver/Groundman	1966
LaVonne	Wolters	Key Punch/Administrative Assistant Engineering	1972–1997
Fr.	Wroblewski	Groundman	1943
Shirley J.	Wurst	Billing Clerk	1956
Philip	Yainske	Groundman	1943
Romuld	Yainske	Groundman	1943
Julian	Yaworsky	Janitor	1951
Berneta H.	Yess	Assistant Cashier	1967
Gregory	Young	PT Line Personnel	1977–1979
Lois J.	Sorenson-Yule	Clerical/Office Service Representative	1961–1984
R.	Zeiner	Groundman	1944
Thomas	Zimmer	Temporary Apprentice Lineman	1992
B. C.	Zimmerman	Groundman	1944
L. P.	Zimmerman	Superintendent	1936
R.	Zimmerman	Groundman	1944

CURRENT EMPLOYEES:

Cindy	Aamot	PT Receptionist/Clerk	2003–present
Justin	Bergeson	Lineman	2007–present
Don	Bos	Relief Crew Chief	1988–present
Syd	Briggs	General Manager	2009–present
Laurie	Burbank	Accounting Assistant	1980–present
Darla	DeVries	Office Division Manager	1985–present
Debbie	Eby	Executive Assistant/VPN Administrator	1997–present
Kathy	Friedrichs	Customer Service Representative	1985–present
Paul	Hanson	Field Supervisor/Construction Engineer	1964, 1965, 1966,1967, 1969, 1971–present

Steele-Waseca's employees pictured in 2010. (*Photo courtesy of Oldenburg Photography.*)

Nordean	Hartle	Assistant Relief Crew Chief	1992–present
Paul	Hoffman	Foreman	1976–present
Doug	Hughes	Marketing Division Manager	1972, 1973–present
Kim	Huxford	Operations Division Manager	1987–present
John	Iverson	Truck Washer/Line Foreman	1967, 1968, 1969–present
Jake	Jacobson	Field Engineer	1985–present
DeAnn	Kaplan	PT Cooperative Assistant	1984–present
Todd	Kubicek	Plant Accountant	1991–present
Dave	Lundberg	Finance Division Manager	1973–present
Mark	McDonald	Member Services Engineer	2000–present
Dan	Meier	Lineman	2000–present
Troy	Pederson	Lineman	1999–present
Tom	Poole	Apprentice Lineman	2008–present
Luke	Ranvek	Lineman	2000–present
Roger	Rehman	Buyer/Storekeeper	1988–present
Kristi	Robinson	Distribution System Engineer	2002–present
Matt	Rohman	Lineman	2007–present
Jack	Schwab	Assistant Relief Crew Chief	1992–present
Randy	Sobrack	Communication Specialist	2009–present
Jon	Stelter	Finance Team Leader	1989–present
Kim	Wilson	Customer Service Representative	1998–present
Jim	Wolters	Crew Chief	1976–present

Bibliography

Cooke, Morris L., "Electrifying the Countryside." *Survey Graphic*. Survey Associates, Inc.; New Deal Net
work. http://newdeal.feri.org/texts/184.htm; pages 2–3.

"Crews lines weren't crossed when baby, mom needed help." *Owatonna People's Press*, Friday,
July 20, 1984.

"A glimpse of things to come." *Steele-Waseca Cooperative Electric: Celebrating the 40th Anniversary of
REA*. Produced for Rural Electric Cooperatives by Church Offset Printing, Inc., Albert Lea, Minnesota,
1976; page 3.

"Line Energized; Sterling Efforts Lauded." *Blooming Prairie Times*, February 10, 1938, pages 1, 8.

Service in the Cooperative Spirit. Annual report for Steele-Waseca Cooperative Electric, 1988;
pages 13–14.

Sparks newsletters produced by Steele-Waseca Cooperative Electric between the periods of May 1940,
November 1940–April 1941, June 1941–August 1952, October 1952–December 2010.

"TVA: Electricity for All." http://newdeal.feri.org/tva/tva10.htm; page 1.

"Waseca Subscribers Review Efforts." *Blooming Prairie Times*, February 10, 1938, page 3.

"Watts" Happening. Annual report for Steele-Waseca Cooperative Electric, 1973; pages 11, 13.

Index

About the Author

Author Randy Sobrack is the communications specialist at Steele-Waseca Cooperative Electric. He joined the co-op in May 2006 through his employment with Manpower in Owatonna. He was formally hired by Steele-Waseca in December 2009.

Randy graduated from Owatonna High School in 1981. He earned a bachelor of science degree in mathematics and a minor in mass communications, along with a teaching certificate, from Mankato State University in 1986.

In the fall of 1986, Sobrack was the secondary math/computer science teacher at Bricelyn Public School. His position was eliminated after the 1986–1987 school year when Bricelyn and Kiester consolidated their school districts. After a year of substitute teaching and other part-time employment, Randy attended the Brown Institute in Minneapolis where he earned certification in television and radio broadcasting in 1989.

Sobrack worked as a news director at WMCW Radio in Harvard, Illinois, and had two stints with KRFO Radio in Owatonna. Between the KRFO stints, Randy was a substitute teacher and spent a few years as a preschool teacher at Kids Korner Educare in Owatonna.

Randy lived in Sleepy Eye with his wife, Holly, and children, Amber and Carson, from 1999 to 2004. During that time, Sobrack was the managing editor at the *Sleepy Eye Herald-Dispatch* and became editor/publisher in 2002. The family has resided in Medford since 2004. ■